THE MODEL RAILROADER'S GUIDE TO
STEEL MILLS

BERNARD KEMPINSKI

KALMBACH BOOKS

Kalmbach Books
21027 Crossroads Circle
Waukesha, Wisconsin 53186
www.Kalmbach.com/Books

Published in 2010
14 13 12 11 10   1 2 3 4 5

Manufactured in the United States of America

ISBN: 978-0-89024-751-8

Unless noted, photos were taken by the author.

Publisher's Cataloging-In-Publication Data

Kempinski, Bernard.
  The model railroader's guide to steel mills / Bernard Kempinski.

  p. : ill. ; cm. -- (Model railroader books)

  ISBN: 978-0-89024-751-8

1. Steel-works--Models--Design and construction. 2. Iron-works--Models--Design and construction.
3. Railroads--Models--Design and construction. 4. Steel-works--History.
5. Iron-works--History. I. Title. II. Title: Steel mills III. Series: Model railroader books.

TF197 .K46 2010
625.19

CONTENTS

Introduction

Flames and smoke belching from stacks is the classic image of early steel mills. This vintage postcard shows a typical scene in a steel mill before the current era of pollution controls. *Author's collection*

Think of a steel mill and you picture smoke, sparks, molten metal, and grimy men working in cavernous, mysterious complexes laced with a bewildering array of pipes, wires, and rail lines radiating in every direction. Perhaps no other industry depends on railroads as much as the steel industry. Railroads transport trainloads of raw materials in and finished product out as well as providing intra-plant movement of intermediary products during nearly every manufacturing step.

This book presents a concise guide to the steel industry and offers track-planning ideas, modeling tips, and techniques for designing and building a rail-served integrated steel mill on a layout. There is enough railroad activity in a steel mill that a satisfying layout can be built just focusing on the mill, and I have included some plans with that approach.

Alternatively, a modeler can include a steel mill as a peripheral industry on a layout and model some of the traffic that flows in and out with perhaps an interchange yard acting as the connection point.

This is an introductory volume and as such cannot cover all the fascinating aspects of modeling the steel industry. The book focuses on the steelmaking process, mill structures, and railroads that support the steel mill. I hope it gives you a taste of the fun available to steel mill modelers. A highly weathered, detailed, and complex industry that hosts intense operations with specialized rail cars is hard to beat in a model railroad. If you are interested in finding out more, I've listed additional resources on page 6.

Basic steel chemistry

Steel is an alloy of iron, carbon, and other trace elements. An alloy is a metallic compound that combines two or more elements. Iron is an element, which means that a piece of pure iron contains iron—and only iron—atoms. Compounds are combinations of elements. A metal combined with oxygen is called an oxide.

Iron ore generally occurs as a form of iron oxide, usually as the mineral compound hematite, although other forms are possible. Most of the world's iron ore deposits were formed under conditions that have not existed on Earth for about 1.8 billion years. While there is still a lot of ancient ore out there in Australia, Brazil, and even Minnesota, nobody's making any more of it.

Iron oxides tend to be weak and flaky. Early metalsmiths learned that they could remove most of the oxygen by heating iron oxide in a pile of burning charcoal, which left elemental iron. To remove the iron from the oxygen, the oxygen must find an element that would have a stronger bond than it has with iron. The strength of a carbon-oxygen bond is greater than that of the iron-oxygen bond. At high temperatures, charcoal is mostly carbon. When iron oxides are heated in charcoal, chemical reactions between carbon and oxygen remove oxygen from

With an array of pipes, wires, beams, and structures, modeling a steel mill can appear to be a daunting task, but it is a fun and rewarding activity. *Library of Congress*

the iron oxide to form carbon dioxide and elemental iron.

Iron has a very high melting temperature (2,800°F), so in a charcoal furnace, it never gets hot enough to liquefy. Removing the oxygen leaves a porous metallic glob that is mostly iron. Early blacksmiths had to repeatedly manipulate the iron when heating and then pound the metal into a sword, shield, plow, or other item. The pounding not only created the desired shape, it drove out slag and other impurities in the iron and helped refine the ore.

Although these early metalsmiths did not know it, the charcoal does more than just remove oxygen from iron oxide. Some carbon atoms from the charcoal get absorbed into the iron to create an iron-carbon alloy. Over centuries of practice, they recognized that there was

a connection between how much charcoal they used or how long they left the iron in contact with the charcoal and how strong the iron was.

Wrought iron, probably the first commonly used iron alloy, was named because it is wrought (worked by repeated hammering) from the porous iron produced by heating iron oxide with charcoal. Wrought iron is much stronger than pure iron even though it is less than 0.15 percent carbon by weight. Part of wrought iron's strength comes from the inclusion of about 1-3 percent silica slag. The slag is also what gives wrought iron a "grain" resembling wood, which is visible when it is etched or bent to the point of failure. The Eiffel Tower is an example of a structure made primarily from wrought iron. Replaced by steel, not much wrought iron is produced anymore.

Waste gas burns from the stack of the Amamda furnace at AK Steel in Ashland, Ky. I was able to take this dramatic photo on public property from outside the mill.

If a small amount of carbon makes iron stronger, more carbon should make iron even stronger. And cast iron, which has between 2 and 4 percent carbon by weight, as well as 1-2 percent silica, is indeed stronger than wrought iron. But there's a trade-off: while the additional carbon makes cast iron stronger, it is also more brittle. Cast iron is easily molded and machined. It resists deformation, wear, and oxidation. It has a wide range of applications, including pipes, stoves, engine blocks, cylinder heads, and gearbox cases.

Steel's carbon content ranges from 0.2 percent to 2.0 percent by weight. Steel's improved properties come about because carbon changes the way the iron atoms arrange themselves in their solid crystalline structure.

The crystal structure of steel-carbon alloys can also be changed even if the alloy is not in a liquid state. As the alloy heats up, the solid crystals rearrange themselves with only small changes in volume. In the iron-carbon alloy, a transformation takes place between about 1,300°F and 1,600°F.

Alternately heating and cooling the alloy at controlled rates can rearrange the crystal structure to create material with desired proper-

ties. This is the principle that allows metallurgists to heat-treat metal to make it harder, tougher, or tempered. Heat from welding can also affect the crystal structure of steel and result in unintended heat-treating and changes in the properties of steel.

It is also possible to alter the crystalline structure and, hence, the strength of steel by permanently changing its overall shape. This is called work hardening and happens when steel is bent or otherwise shaped. When steel is cold rolled, there is a limit to how much work hardening steel can take before it fails. To avoid work hardening, rolling mills tend to shape steel while it is red hot.

For more information

In researching steel mills over the past 15 years, I have found that public libraries contain a wealth of information on the economics of steel and labor relations but very little on mill operations. The Internet offers better results. Several corporations have very informative Web sites, particularly AK Steel (www.aksteel.com) and the American Iron and Steel Institute (www. steel.org). There is an active Yahoo group dedicated to HO steel mill modeling, which you may find worth joining.

The Historical Architectural and Engineering Record (HAER) at the Library of Congress has a great collection of material concerning significant defunct steel mills across the country. Various HAER photos and diagrams can be seen in this book, but many more are available online. Historical societies and other organizations have good collections of steel mill images, such as the Calumet Regional Archives at Indiana University Northwest (www.iun.edu/~cra). Sites providing aerial images are also useful to contemporary modelers.

While rare, the opportunity does exist for touring a steel mill. I was able to arrange an official tour of a mill, and its highlight was an impressive steel-pouring operation at the basic oxygen furnace. You can also view the activities of various steel mills across the country from public property outside the mills. I have made trips to several of these sites, and they proved invaluable for learning about small details and seeing the clutter that populates a typical steel mill.

I would recommend the following books on the steel industry:

The Making, Shaping, and Treating of Steel was regularly issued during various time periods by U.S. Steel.

Blast Furnace Construction in America by J. E. Johnson was written in 1917 and is a great early reference.

Steel: The Diary of a Furnace Worker by Charles Rumford Walker, 1922, offers an engaging story about life in early steel mills.

The Blast Furnaces of Sparrows Point: One Hundred Years of Ironmaking on the Chesapeake Bay by John Lovis provides an inside look at steel mills in a more recent era, complete with many maps, diagrams, and charts.

Dean Freytag has written two books on steel mill modeling, and they are worth adding to your library if you can find them, as they are out of print. They are *The History, Making, and Modeling of Steel* (recently reprinted by NMRA) and *The Cyclopedia of Industrial Modeling*.

For additional modeling ideas see Jeff Bourne's *Superdetailing a Walthers Blast Furnace* DVDs (Part 1 and Part 2) offered by PrairieWorks (www.prairie-works.com).

History of steel

1-1

ONE

Steel is such an integral part of the modern society that it is hard to imagine life without plentiful steel, **1-1**. But as late as 150 years ago, steel was a relatively scarce material reserved for critical applications such as weapons and armor. Although man has known about steel for several thousand years, archeologists are not sure when it was first discovered; the means to produce it were not easy.

The bloomery technique of making iron started the Iron Age. The first discovery probably came when a lump of iron ore in a particularly hot fire led to a strange material left in the embers of the fire. From this, the bloomery furnace developed to produce a small lump of poor-quality wrought iron from a mixture of iron ore and charcoal assisted by a blast of air from hand-worked bellows, and it was enough to make an impact on history.

Two steam switching engines work the tracks at the Republic Steel mill in Cleveland. Founded in 1899 as Republic Steel and Iron Company, Republic Steel at one time was the third-largest steel producer in the United States. *Library of Congress, HAER*

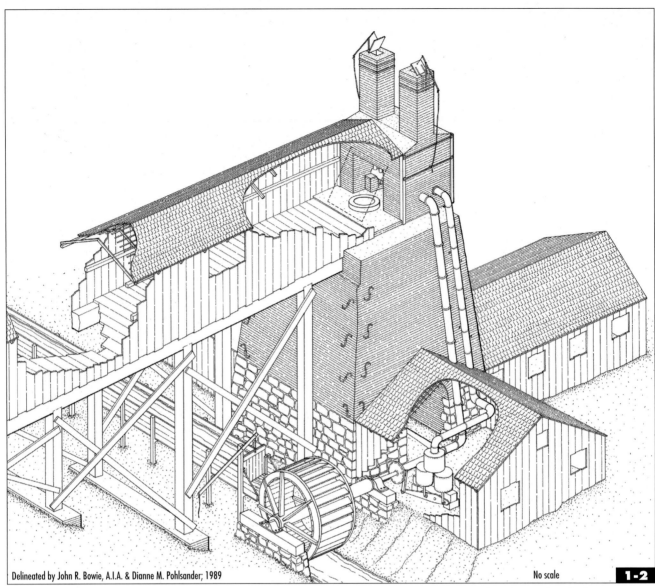

No scale **1-2**

This typical, early American blast furnace (around 1807-1830) was built at Nassawango, Md. The elevated platform at the left allows easier loading at the charging hole and at the water wheel to power the blowers. This furnace relied on bog iron ore from nearby Nassawango Creek, which had an iron concentration of 51 percent. *Library of Congress, HAER*

During the Middle Ages, smiths began to increase the efficiency and the size of bloomeries. Taller furnaces and the tuyere (pronounced twee-air), a nozzle to increase the velocity of the blast air, were some of the early innovations. Eventually, furnaces became so tall that human-powered leather bellows could not produce a strong enough blast, so smiths used waterpower to compress air into a stronger blast, which required that furnaces be located near waterways. As innovators added improvements one by one, medieval blast furnace technology emerged.

The discovery of cast iron was somewhat of an accident as early smiths regarded it as a waste product because it could not be wrought (worked). Nevertheless, cast iron proved to be a very useful product. No single date or place is accepted for this discovery, but true blast furnaces needed for cast iron production were observed as early as 1150 in Europe.

American beginnings

Because of the difficulty in transporting raw materials, early American smelters located furnaces near the sources of iron ore, **1-2**. They tended to be in rural locations surrounded by thick native forests that provided charcoal. Small villages grew around the furnaces, and an entire settlement would resemble an industrial plantation.

America had plentiful forests, so it was not until the 1840s and 1850s that coal replaced charcoal in iron furnaces. Because anthracite was found in the settled areas of the new country, especially eastern Pennsylvania, and is almost pure carbon, it was the first type of coal used. It was difficult to get anthracite coal to burn, but smelters learned to use hot blast air instead of cold air for better burning. To improve furnace efficiency, smelters adopted regenerative heating of the blast air using hot waste gas from the blast furnace combustion, **1-3**. Early heat

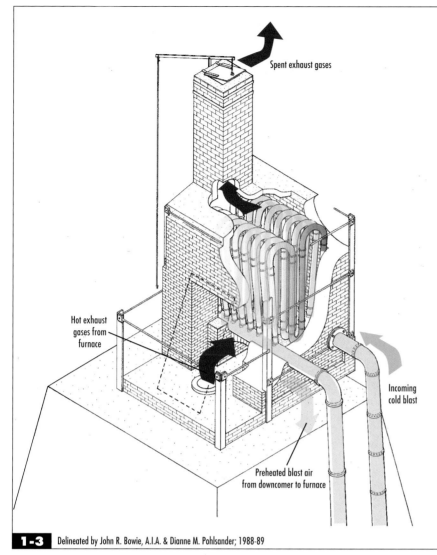

The ruins of the Eliza blast furnace in Cambria County, Pa., still have the remains of the heat exchangers at the top. The pipe visible on the face of the furnace is the cold blast line from the air pumps. The wooden chimneys and other parts are long gone. *Library of Congress, HAER*

Spent exhaust gases

Hot exhaust gases from furnace

Incoming cold blast

Preheated blast air from downcomer to furnace

1-3 Delineated by John R. Bowie, A.I.A. & Dianne M. Pohlsander; 1988-89

The works at the top of the blast furnace at Nassawango are an early example of heat exchangers for heating the blast air with waste heat from the iron refining process. *Library of Congress, HAER*

exchangers that preheated the blast air were simple arrangements of pipes at the top of the blast furnace, **1-4**. Later, steelmakers added scrubbers and washers to clean the hot, corrosive exhaust gases to allow the use of elaborate regenerative brick-lined stoves.

Anthracite coal did not crush as easily as charcoal when loaded in the furnace and was less likely to clog up the blast. Thus anthracite-fueled ironworks could be larger, more efficient, and more profitable. For about a decade, ironworks sprang up in Pennsylvania near the anthracite coalfields. By the close of the Civil War, however, American steelmakers adopted the British practice of using

coke derived from bituminous coal. This coal was located in many parts of the country, and the next generation of blast furnaces sprang up near the coking fields south of Pittsburgh, **1-5**.

Blast furnaces were now exclusively making pig iron, which has a relatively high carbon content (4-5 percent) and is very brittle. Some pig iron was used to make cast iron, but the majority of pig iron produced by blast furnaces underwent further processing to reduce the carbon content and to form various grades of wrought iron or steel.

Puddling

Puddling was the first true industrial process to make low-carbon wrought iron from pig iron that came from blast

furnaces, **1-6**. The puddling furnace directed heated air from a fire, which was physically separated from the hearth, over the iron without it coming into direct contact with the fuel; thereby, keeping impurities in the fuel away from the iron. This type of arrangement is also known as a reverberatory furnace, **1-7**. Solid pig iron was heated vigorously in the hearth until it was entirely molten. The ironmaker had to manually stir, or "puddle," the pig iron with long bars, **1-8**, which were consumed in the process, bringing the pig iron into contact with oxygen in the air and burning off any surplus carbon.

The iron began to solidify as the carbon was removed. Eventually the worker manipulated the wrought iron into a single lump of iron in the center of the hearth, **1-9**. This was a physically exhausting job that required skill and experience to do correctly. Although, in theory, this was wrought iron, it was not usable in this form because of the extensive slag within the lump. To remove the slag, the worker lifted the lump from the furnace and repeatedly hammered it. This was a dangerous job, as with each drop of the hammer, white-hot slag would spread out across the forge. After the excess slag was removed, the iron was rolled into bars or sheets.

1-5

The 60-foot-tall Lucy Selina blast furnace of the Longdale Iron Company near Clifton Forge, Va., featured a hot blast pipe, a 3-foot narrow gauge railway, and an early type of inclined skip hoist. *Lane/Schnepf collection*

Cementation

Cementation was another laborious and time-consuming process that converted wrought iron into blister steel. The process created a blistered surface appearance on the steel bars when they were removed from the furnace. By heating wrought iron surrounded by charcoal for about a week's time, the cementation process added carbon back to the wrought iron to make mild steel.

During the long, slow heating, the iron bars absorbed carbon from the charcoal. The blisters formed as result of uneven carbon absorption. These surface blisters contained steel with a high carbon content while the centers of the bars were still wrought iron that contained very little carbon because carbon does not diffuse readily through solid iron. Because of this uneven composition, blister steel had to be processed further. The smith heated the blister steel and forged it under a hammer until the bar was folded over on itself, which blended the steel and

1-6

The B&O Railroad established a rail rolling mill in Cumberland, Md., in 1869 to exploit the nearby reserves of coal and iron. The mill initially used pig iron from the Bowery furnace in Frostburg in its 12 puddling furnaces. The mill rolled rail and other shapes using three sets of rollers as well as steam-driven saws and hammers. The mill was closed in 1888 but reopened under Cambria Iron Company and became Cumberland Iron. It was torn down in 1981. *Library of Congress, HAER*

unrefined iron. Additional rounds of folding and hammering produced higher grades of steel.

Bessemer process

The Bessemer process revolutionized steelmaking. Named after its inventor, Henry Bessemer, who patented it in 1855, it was the first inexpensive industrial process for the mass production of steel from molten pig iron.

The key principle is the removal of impurities, such as silicon, manganese, and excess carbon, from the iron by oxidation through air being blown through the molten iron. These oxides either escaped as gas or formed solid slag. Oxygen from the air blast combined with the excess carbon to form carbon monoxide, thus reducing the carbon content of the pig iron to desired levels. The oxidation also raised the temperature of the iron mass and kept it molten. Each batch took about 30 minutes to process and ranged from 5 to 30 tons.

The Bessemer converter is a large steel vessel supported on pivots, **1-10**. It has a large opening in the top in the form of a spout. The flat bottom of the converter has a number of openings through which air blows during the conversion process.

To charge the converter, workmen tipped it onto its back and poured molten iron in through the upturned spout. They also added scrap iron and steel to keep the reaction temperature down. Then they rotated it to the upright working position while applying slight air pressure. With the spout upright, and sometimes aligned to a duct or chimney to carry the smoke and fumes out of the building, the conversion process began. The air pressure was increased until it moved vigorously through the molten iron and created a spectacular shower of flames and sparks. The process was difficult to control, and the quality of the steel varied. When ready, workers reduced the blast as they tilted the furnace to pour out the contents, a process called teeming.

The basic Bessemer process was a major refinement. It removed phosphorous from the iron by using an alkali (basic) lining in the vessel. This allowed

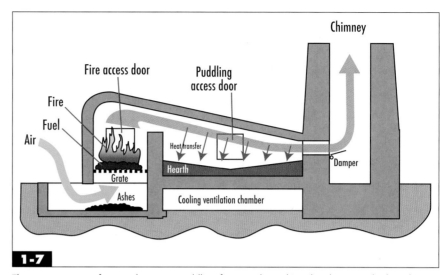

This cross section of a reverberatory puddling furnace shows how the charge in the hearth is heated by hot gases passing over the hearth (a convective heat transfer) and by heat radiating from the hot oven walls.

U.S. Labor Secretary James "Puddler Jim" Davis demonstrates his puddling technique to two ironworkers around 1921. Davis was an American steelworker and politician from Pittsburgh, who eventually served in the U.S. Senate. *Library of Congress*

A worker uses an iron bar to manipulate the iron blob, called a loup, in a puddling furnace. Amazingly, he doesn't wear any protective clothing. Slag drips out the bottom of the access door. *Library of Congress*

1-10

A Bessemer converter in action. The airflow from the bottom creates a shower of flame and sparks. Trying to simulate this action would be an interesting challenge on a model railroad. *Library of Congress*

1-11

First established in 1881, Irondale is significant as the site of one of the first attempts to introduce heavy industry into western Washington. In 1906, the Irondale Furnace Company purchased the property and later, as Western Steel Corporation, added a full-scale steel plant. Irondale, unique during this era, was the only plant west of Pueblo, Colo., to produce steel from its own raw materials. *Library of Congress, HAER*

the wide use of lower quality iron ores in producing steel.

Two 5-ton Bessemer plants were operating in the United States by 1866, but the need to ship pig iron in bars from remote furnaces and then remelt them in small furnaces limited daily output.

The efficiency of the Bessemer furnace could be increased with the use of pure oxygen. Air is mostly nitrogen and only about 20 percent oxygen, and the nitrogen in the air blast could make the steel brittle and less malleable. In Bessemer's time, pure oxygen was not available as a commercial tonnage product, so improved quality and efficiency from using pure oxygen had to wait until development of the basic oxygen system after World War II.

Two engineers, Charles William Siemens and Pierre-Émile Martin, working separately, developed another method of converting iron to steel at about the same time as Bessemer. In the Siemens-Martin process, steel was produced either by melting pig iron in the hearth of a reverberatory furnace and adding wrought iron until the molten metal attained the desired degree of carbonization or by mixing cast iron with certain kinds of iron ores. The process competed with Bessemer in price, but problems in developing a commercial reverberatory furnace that could withstand the high heat needed to melt the iron delayed the adoption of the Siemens-Martin process until much later.

With the Bessemer process, cheap steel became readily available, which modernized other industries and helped bring about the industrial revolution, **1-11**. The influence railroads had on the steel industry was immense. The rise of rail transportation was probably the most important factor in the fast growth of the Bessemer steel process. Railroads made it possible to cheaply move raw materials from rural iron plantations to cities where capital, labor, and markets were abundant.

Moreover, railroads themselves were an enormous market for iron and steel products—rails, rolling stock, girders, and bridges being only a few of the items needed. In order to ensure adequate supplies of steel, railroad officials promoted, funded, and even founded early Bessemer steel works. As steel rail became stronger, trains got bigger, engines became more powerful, and loads increased.

At the turn of the 20th century, a naval arms race between the world powers pushed the steel industry forward. High-powered weapons and armor plate required more advanced steel formulations. Defense departments around the world provided the impetus for advances in steel research and manufacture. Steel also played a major part in municipal and civil construction. Steel frames for buildings made skyscrapers possible, permanently altering the look of city skylines.

Ironmaking

2-1

Just before the start of the 20th century, the integrated steel mill became the dominant mode of steel manufacturing. An integrated steel mill takes raw materials in the form of ore, coal, and scrap and produces finished steel products, **2-1**. Essential tasks of an integrated mill include melting and refining iron ore into pig iron, making coke, converting pig iron to steel, and casting and rolling steel into finished products, **2-2**.

Andrew Carnegie was one of the first steel tycoons to integrate his steel mills both vertically, by owning or controlling all his raw material suppliers and steel fabricators, as well as horizontally by consolidating the facilities into one location. Henry Ford took this idea one step further when he colocated a steel mill and an automobile manufacturing plant at the famous River Rouge plant in Dearborn, Mich.

The Jones and Laughlin Steel Company in Aliquippa, Pa., on the Ohio River is a good example of an integrated steel mill, with multiple blast furnaces, coke works, rolling mills, and other support structures. *Library of Congress*

Steel mills in the U. S. and Canada

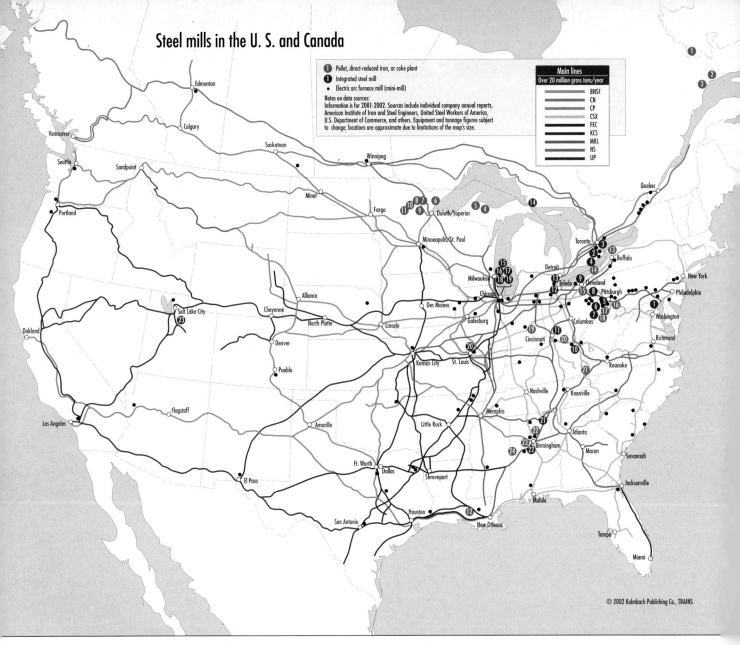

① Pellet, direct-reduced iron, or coke plant
① Integrated steel mill
• Electric arc furnace mill (mini-mill)

Notes on data sources:
Information is for 2001-2002. Sources include individual company annual reports,
American Institute of Iron and Steel Engineers, United Steel Workers of America,
U.S. Department of Commerce, and others. Equipment and tonnage figures subject
to change; locations are approximate due to limitations of the map's size.

Main lines
Over 20 million gross tons/year

BNSF
CN
CP
CSX
FEC
KCS
MRL
NS
UP

© 2002 Kalmbach Publishing Co., TRAINS

U.S. and Canadian integrated steel mills

Name	Location	Annual capacity (million tons), equipment, notes
1. Bethlehem Steel, Sparrows Point	Sparrows Point, Md.	3.7 1 blast furnace, 2 BOFs (filed bankruptcy 10/15/01)
2. Dofasco, Hamilton Operation	Hamilton, Ont.	4.0 3 blast furnaces, 1 BOF, 1 EAF, 246 coke ovens
3. Stelco, Hilton Works	Hamilton, Ont.	3.0 2 blast furnaces, 3 BOFs, 83 coke ovens
4. Lake Erie Steel, division of Stelco	Nanticoke, Ont.	2.3 1 blast furnace, 2 BOFs, 45 coke ovens
5. U.S. Steel, Edgar Thomson Plant	Braddock, Pa.	2.8 2 blast furnaces, 2 BOFs
6. Weirton Steel, Weirton Plant	Weirton, W. Va.	3.0 2 blast furnaces, 2 BOFs
7. Wheeling-Pittsburgh Steel, Steubenville Plant	Steubenville, Ohio	2.4 2 blast furnaces, 2 BOFs, 224 coke ovens (filed bankruptcy 11/16/00)
8. WCI Steel, Warren Plant	Warren, Ohio	1.5 1 blast furnace, 2 BOFs
9. International Steel, Cleveland Works	Cleveland, Ohio	3.0 2 blast furnaces, 4 BOFs (formerly LTV Steel)
10. AK Steel, Ashland Works	Ashland, Ky.	2.1 1 blast furnace, 2BOFs, 146 coke ovens
11. AK Steel, Middletown Works	Middletown, Ohio	2.3 1 blast furnace, 2 BOFs, 76 coke ovens
12. National Steel, Great Lakes Operations	Ecorse, Mich.	3.5 3 blast furnaces, 2 BOFs, 85 coke ovens (filed bankruptcy 03/06/02)
13. Rouge Steel, Rouge Plant	Dearborn, Mich.	3.3 2 blast furnaces, 2 BOFs
14. Algoma Steel, Steelworks Division	Sault Ste. Marie, Ont.	2.5 1 blast furnace, 2 BOFs, 177 coke ovens
15. Bethlehem Steel, Burns Harbor	Burns Harbor, Ind.	5.0 2 blast furnaces, 3 BOFs, 164 coke ovens
16. U.S. Steel, Gary Works	Gary, Ind.	7.7 4 blast furnaces, 6 BOFs, 268 coke ovens
17. Ispat Inland, Indiana Harbor Works	East Chicago, Ind.	5.8 3 blast furnaces, 2 BOFs
18. International Steel, Indiana Harbor Works	East Chicago, Ind.	3.7 3 blast furnaces, 2 BOFs, 60 coke ovens (formerly LTV Steel)
19. Acme Steel, Chicago and Riverdale Plants	Riverdale, Ill.	1.2 2 blast furnaces, 2 BOFs, 100 coke ovens (ceased operations 10/25/01)
20. National Steel, Granite City	Granite City, Ill.	2.5 2 blast furnaces, 2 BOFs, 90 coke ovens
21. Gulf States Steel, Gadsden Plant	Gadsden, Ala.	1.1 2 blast furnaces, 2 BOFs, 130 coke ovens (ceased operations 08/21/00)
22. U.S. Steel, Fairfield Works	Fairfield, Ala.	2.3 1 blast furnace, 3 BOFs
23. Geneva Steel, Geneva Works	Vineyard, Utah	2.5 3 blast furnaces, 2 BOFs, 197 coke ovens (ceased operations 11/14/01)

Note: BOF = basic oxygen furnace, EAF = electric arc furnace, DRI = direct-reduced iron

U.S. and Canadian taconite pellet, direct-reduced iron, and coke plants

Name	Location	Annual capacity (million tons)	
1. Iron Ore of Canada	Labrador City, Nfld.	15.0	
2. Wabush Mines	Pointe-Noire, Que.	6.0	
3. Quebec Cartier Mining	Port Cartier, Que.	8.2	
4. Empire Iron Mining	Palmer, Mich.	8.0	
5. Tilden Mining	Ishpeming, Mich.	7.8	
6. Northshore Mining	Silver Bay, Minn.	4.7	pellets
7. Ispat Inland Mining	Virginia, Minn.	5.4	
8. U.S. Steel Minntac	Mountain Iron, Mich.	16.2	
9. EVTAC Mining	Forbes, Minn.	5.4	
10. Hibbing Taconite	Hibbing, Minn.	8.3	
11. National Steel Pellet	Keewatin, Minn.	5.3	
12. American Iron Reduction	Convent, La.	1.5 (closed 10/01) -DRI	
13. Tonawanda Coke	Tonawanda, N.Y.	0.23	
14. Erie Coke	Erie, Pa.	0.20	
15. ISG, Warren Coke Plant	Warren, Ohio	0.50 (formerly LTV)	
16. Shenango	Pittsburgh, Pa.	0.35	
17. U.S. Steel, Clairton Works	Clairton, Pa,	4.70	
18. Koppers Industries	Monessen, Pa.	0.94	coke
19. Citizens Gas & Coal Utility	Indianapolis, Ind.	0.60	
20. New Boston Coke	Portsmouth, Ohio	0.35	
21. Jewell Coal & Coke	Vansant, Va.	0.75	
22. ABC Coke	Tarrant City, Ala.	0.60	
23. Sloss Industries	Birmingham, Ala.	0.37	
24. Empire Coke	Holt, Ala.	0.13	

Not all mills are integrated. Some facilities perform only one function and ship the intermediate product to other locations. These are called merchant mills. Foundries are examples of stand-alone works that take pig iron and make finished products. Coke is another product commonly made in merchant-type works, **2-3**.

The first integrated mills sprung up in the 1880s using Bessemer steel technology. A typical integrated steel mill featured one or more blast furnaces, a coke works, several Bessemer convert-ers, an ingot-casting facility, and rolling mills. It also had support structures such as storage tanks, ore bridges, cranes, power stations, and offices to keep it running. Open hearths became widely used in the 1890s. By 1900, most of Carnegie's steel came from open hearths. By the 1930s, open-hearth furnaces made Bessemer converters obsolete, and the last Bessemer furnace in North America went out of commis-sion in the 1960s. After 1990, basic oxygen furnaces replaced the open hearth, while continuous casters replaced the ingot-casting operation.

In the 1980s, there were 50 inte-grated steel mills in the United States; today, there are about 20 concentrated in the Great Lakes region (see map from *Trains* magazine on opposite page). As integrated mills close down, mini-mills are becoming more numerous. A mini-mill is a steelmaking facility without a

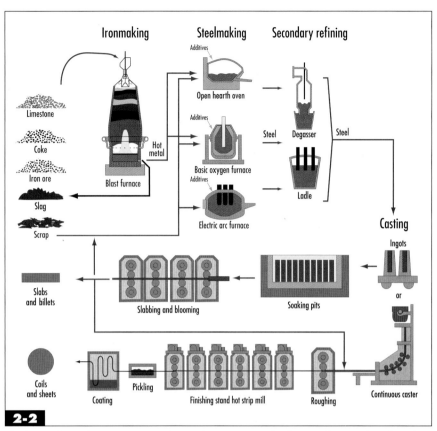

This figure shows the major steps in the production process for the manufacture of steel products at an integrated steel mill.

blast furnace, but it has an electric arc furnace. Mini-mills make steel from scrap, pig iron, and some ore. (They are discussed more in the next chapter.)

We'll focus mainly on steel mills from the early 1930s to the present, such as the Republic Steel mill in Cleveland, **2-4**, as these are probably of

most interest to the scale modeler thanks to the Walthers blast furnace kit, which is appropriate for this time period. Modeling buildings from earlier eras is possible through scratchbuilding, and the resulting smaller structures are easier to fit in the typical space available to model railroaders, **2-5**.

The U.S. Steel Clairton works is still in operation as a merchant coke operation. *Library of Congress, HAER*

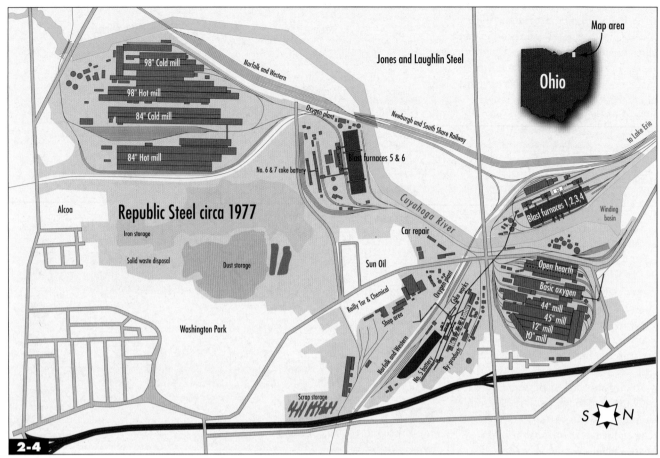

Republic Steel spreads out along the Cuyahoga River in Cleveland. The widely spaced facilities would translate into an interesting model railroad design as intra-plant moves could be located in different parts of the layout room with longer-than-usual switching moves between them.

This 1920s aerial photo shows the merchant blast furnace at Low Moor, Va. The furnace was built in 1880 and rebuilt in 1910 to a height of 80 feet with a 19-foot-tall hearth. It had an annual output of 130,000 tons. For steam modelers, a facility like this would make a manageable project. *C&O Historical Society*

Raw materials

In 1997, blast furnaces in the United States produced 54.7 million short tons of iron. Iron ore, coke, and limestone flux are the primary materials in iron production. Producing a ton of iron from a blast furnace requires 1.7 tons of iron ore, 950 to 1,300 pounds of coke, 550 pounds of flux, and 1.6 to 2.0 tons of air.

Iron ore, in the form of raw ore, pellets, or sinter, is the primary source of iron for integrated steel mills. To be used, raw ore must be 50-70 percent iron. Lower-grade iron ore can be used, but it must be concentrated, usually in the form of taconite pellets, to increase its iron content.

Sinter is produced from very fine raw ore, coke, sand-sized limestone particles, and other steel-plant scrap materials that contain some iron, which otherwise might go to waste. It cannot be used in the blast furnace without processing, as its small size would cause the furnace to clog. The fine particles get mixed together in proper proportion and sent into the sintering furnace on a steel conveyor belt. There, they get fused into larger-sized pieces that are suitable for a blast furnace.

Normally in an integrated mill, coke is made on-site. The coke ovens are usually the biggest emitter of air pollutants at a steel mill. With strict air pollution controls now in place, many mills have closed their on-site coke ovens and purchase their coke from a merchant coke producer that uses the latest pollution-control equipment.

Used as flux, the final raw material in the ironmaking process is limestone. Flux is a general name for any material used in the iron- or steelmaking process that collects impurities from molten metal.

The blast furnace

A blast furnace is the first stop in producing steel from iron ore. Blast furnace equipment is in continuous evolution, and modern, giant furnaces can produce 13,000 tons per day. The blast furnace is the signature structure of an integrated steel mill, **2-6**. It is worth understanding more about how a blast furnace works to help guide your modeling efforts. A blast furnace is a complex facility and is difficult to model. Starting with the Walthers blast furnace kit (no. 933-3249) is a good shortcut, but even that kit is a complex model. By knowing what the various parts do and how they work, you will be more likely to make a model that looks right.

The purpose of a blast furnace is to chemically reduce and physically convert iron oxides into liquid iron (hot metal), **2-7**. Modern blast furnaces are tall steel vessels lined with heat-resistant refractory brick. The furnaces range in size from 23 to 45 feet in diameter and from 100 to 300 feet tall. Conveyor systems of carts, skip hoists, and ladles carry inputs and outputs to and from the blast furnace.

Once the operators fire up the blast furnace, it runs continuously with only minor interruptions for maintenance until the lining is worn away. The steel industry calls this a campaign, and it can last 7 to 10 years. The operators add coke, iron materials, and flux into the top of the furnace. The raw

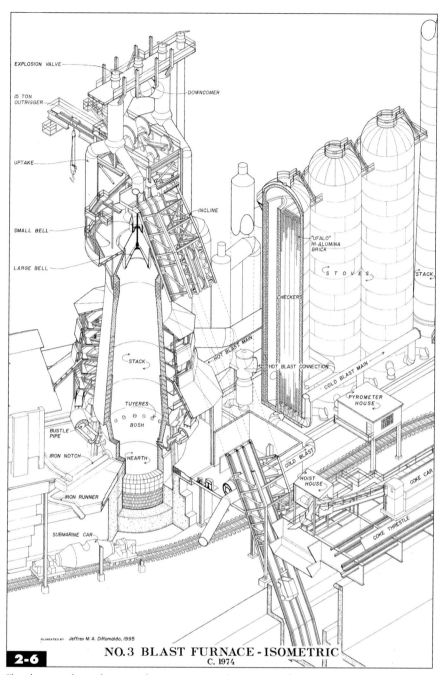

2-6 This drawing shows the general arrangement and pipe routing for the No. 3 blast furnace at Monessen works. This furnace has uptakes that are similar to those on the Walthers blast furnace kit. The uptakes are an important visual aspect of the blast furnace. The Historic American Engineering Record (HAER) has a very detailed set of drawings of this steel mill. *Library of Congress, HAER*

materials take about 6 to 8 hours to descend to the bottom of the furnace where they become the final product of liquid slag and liquid iron. High-pressure hot air flows into the furnace from the bottom through the tuyeres. The hot air ignites the coke, which provides the fuel to melt the iron. As the iron ore melts, chemical reactions occur. Coke releases carbon as it burns, which combines with the iron. Flux combines with the impurities in molten iron to form slag. Slag separates from the molten iron and rises to the surface. The blast furnace operator may blend different types of fluxing stone to produce the desired slag chemistry and create optimum slag properties such as a low melting point and high fluidity.

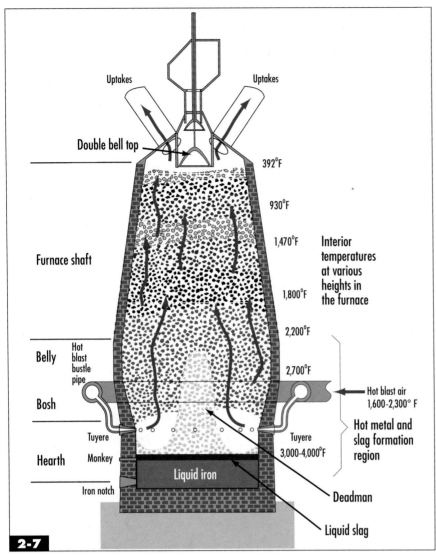

Uptakes

Uptakes

Double bell top

392°F

930°F

1,470°F

Interior temperatures at various heights in the furnace

Furnace shaft

1,800°F

2,200°F

2,700°F

Belly

Hot blast bustle pipe

Bosh

← Hot blast air 1,600-2,300° F

Hot metal and slag formation region

Tuyere

Tuyere 3,000-4,000°F

Hearth

Monkey

Liquid iron

Iron notch

Deadman

Liquid slag

2-7

This cross section of a blast furnace shows the iron-refining process. Raw materials—iron ore, coke, and limestone—enter through the double bell apparatus at the top. Preheated combustion air enters through the tuyeres near the bottom, passes through the contents, and exits the uptakes. The yellow slug in the bottom center is a crucial area of incandescent permeable coke called the "deadman," where the actual melting occurs.

The operators on the cast house floor tap the blast furnace at a level to drain the 3,000°F molten iron, **2-8**. The opening in the furnace hearth for casting or draining the furnace is called the iron notch. Modern, larger blast furnaces may have as many as four iron notches and two cast houses. A taphole drill mounted on a pivoting base swings up to the iron notch and drills a hole through the refractory clay plug, sealing the iron notch, and continues into the liquid iron.

In some furnaces, another opening on the furnace, called the cinder notch or "monkey," is used to draw off excess slag or iron. The workers open this hole to drain excess slag, a process they call

"flushing the monkey." They use an iron poker bar to break the encrusted slag in the hole, so the slag drains out.

With the iron notch drilled open, liquid iron begins to flow down a deep trench called a trough or runner. As the flow of hot metal tapers off, slag starts to emerge from the tap. The workers on the cast house floor use gates and skimmers to route the slag for removal. The skimmers are refractory blocks that sit astride the trough with small openings underneath. The hot metal flows through the skimmer opening and down the iron runners. Since the slag is less dense than iron, it floats on top of the iron down the

trough, hits the skimmer, and gets diverted along a different path into the slag runners.

The hot metal flows through the runners in the cast house floor to specially designed railroad cars called hot metal cars. There are several types of hot metal cars, including pot, ladle, Pollock, submarine, and bottle cars. These cars have refractory-brick linings to insulate the carbody from hot metal and to reduce cooling. Locomotives haul the full cars to a remote slag dump, where the molten slag is dumped, cooled, and crushed for use in industrial processes and roadbuilding.

In some furnaces, the slag flows directly to a pit near the furnace, where it cools before being removed, **2-9**. Recently, large wheeled slag carriers have been replacing rail-mounted slag cars.

When the liquid in the furnace drops down to the iron-notch level, some of the blast sputters and spurts out of the taphole. This signals the end of the cast. The workers reduce the air blast pressure "to take the wind off" the furnace. They swing a mud gun into the iron notch and engage a steam ram to inject refractory clay into the iron notch and stop the flow of liquids, **2-10**.

The hot blast air passing through the tuyeres takes about 10 seconds after going through numerous chemical reactions to reach the top. These gases exit the top of the blast furnace into the uptakes and downcomer, **2-11**. The uptakes, offtakes, and downcomer are large, distinctive pipes that give the blast furnace its visual identity, **2-12**. The hot, dirty gas exits the furnace dome, flows through the uptakes, and then merges into offtakes. The two offtakes then change the direction of the gas downward, merging and routing it to the downcomer. At the extreme top of the uptakes, bleeder valves may release gas and protect the top of the furnace from sudden gas pressure surges.

The gas descends in the downcomer first to the dust catcher, where coarse particles settle out, accumulate, and get periodically dumped into a railroad car or truck for disposal. The gas then flows through a venturi scrubber that removes the finer particles and goes into a gas cooler, where spraying water reduces the temperature of the hot but clean gas. Some modern furnaces are equipped with a combined scrubber and cooling unit.

The cleaned and cooled gas has a considerable energy value, so it is used as fuel to heat the cold blast or to power steam boilers. Through a system of reversible pipes and refractory bricks, the stoves alternately heat up and then release the heat to the air entering the blast furnace to preheat the air and create the hot blast. Some of the excess gas flows to the boiler house to generate steam to power a turbo blower. The turbo blower generates the compressed air (cold blast) that goes to the stoves. All of this gas cleaning, routing, and switching requires piping, valves, and fixtures that make the blast furnace such a challenge to model (see photo on page 5).

The gas flow in a modern blast furnace can be quite complex as gases are cleaned, recycled, and mixed in a myriad of possible combinations. The clean gas pipeline is directed to the hot blast stove. There are usually three or four cylindrically shaped stoves in a line adjacent to the blast furnace. The number of stoves depends on the preferences of the mill designer. The gas burns in the bottom of a stove, and the heat rises and transfers to refractory brick inside the stove. The products of combustion flow through passages in these bricks and out of the stove into a high stack, which all the stoves share, although older designs had stacks on each stove.

A blower, usually located in a separate building, provides the large volume of air, from 80,000 to 230,000 cubic feet per minute, needed for combustion, **2-13**. This air flows through the cold blast main to the stoves. This cold blast then enters the stove that has been previously heated and flows through the heated refractory bricks. Heat stored in the brick transfers from the cold blast to form the hot blast. The hot blast temperature can range from 1,600°F to 2,300°F.

This heated air then exits the stove into the hot blast main that runs to the furnace bustle pipe, a doughnut-shaped

2-8

The blast furnace cast house floor is a busy place. Note the steel plates covering the runners and the overall level of clutter in this busy spot. *Library of Congress, HAER*

2-9

Slag flows to the slag pit adjacent to the cast house at Republic Steel works in Cleveland in the 1940s. *Library of Congress, HAER*

2-10

Workers close a blast furnace tap using the mud gun. Note the lack of protective clothing worn by the workers in this 1940s photo. *Library of Congress*

2-11

The uptakes on this blast furnace at U.S. Steel's Etna works are of an older design common during the 1920s. *Library of Congress*

2-12

Chuck Pravlik backdated the uptakes with numerous pieces of Plastruct tubing and parts on his Walthers model kit to reflect an older blast furnace. *Chuck Pravlik*

2-13

The interior of the blower house at U.S. Steel, Clairton, Pa. The reciprocating blowers are essentially large air compressors that pressurize the blast air. Usually one building houses the blowers for all the blast furnaces in the mill. To power the blowers, boilers create steam by burning excess clean furnace gas, augmented with natural gas or fuel oil. *Library of Congress, HAER*

pipe that encircles the furnace, **2-14**. Before the hot main reaches the bustle pipe, there is usually a mixer line connecting the cold blast main to the hot blast main. A valve on the mixer line allows blending of the two airstreams to control the blast temperature and keep it constant. The mixed blast air enters the bustle pipe and flows into the furnace through tuyeres that are equally spaced around the circumference of the furnace. There may be 14 copper, water-cooled tuyeres on a small blast furnace and 40 tuyeres on a large blast furnace. Oil, tar, natural gas, powdered coal, and oxygen can also be injected into the furnace at tuyere level to increase the input energy if additional productivity is needed.

Prior to the 1950s, there were no process control devices on a blast furnace to monitor the operation. Workers learned to judge the condition of the furnace by indirect methods. For example, peep sights built into the tuyeres allowed the workers to see a small area inside the furnace and make adjustments if they saw slag build up or movement of the incandescent coke. They watched the color and amount of flames jetting from the gaps between the steel plates of the blast furnace. Increased flames could mean that the furnace was going cold, and color

changes could indicate water leakage into the furnace.

Furnaces did not always run smoothly. Uneven materials or unaccounted moisture in the charge could cause uneven gas flow in the furnace. If the materials did not evenly descend down the furnace, they might hang in an unstable position, and at some point, they would suddenly release (called a slip) and drop tons of material, which could force slag into tuyeres and cause a large gas bubble to rise to the top. The bleeder valve on the top of the uptakes could pop open and release dust, flame, and a large gas cloud. In a bad slip, solid material could erupt from the bleeders and rain down on the mill, or worse, the furnace could rupture and cause major damage and injuries. Operators could shake a furnace by turning off the blast and then turning it back on. Repeated shaking could help settle a hanging charge and get the furnace running smoothly again. Workers would feel the whole cast house floor rumble as the hanging material dropped.

Most mills have an ore storage yard to stockpile materials for later use, **2-15**. For example, mills that rely on ore delivered from Great Lakes bulk carriers may have to stockpile ore for use in the winter when ice prevents the ships from sailing. The materials

typically stored in the ore yard include raw ore, pellets, sinter, limestone or flux blend, and possibly coke.

Mills transfer ore from the stockyard to the furnaces in a variety of ways, **2-16**. Ore bridges traverse up and down some yards to move materials with grab buckets, **2-17**, or they can unload ships at waterfront mills. Some newer mills have replaced the ore bridge with conveyor systems, **2-18**. Most blast furnaces have a stock house, high line, and either a skip hoist or conveyor for moving materials to the top of the furnace. The high line is an elevated rail line with storage hoppers underneath that hold and weigh materials.

When it is time to use the materials, the ore bridges or conveyor belts transfer materials to the stock house, which is located at the bottom of the skip hoist. Materials can also arrive at the stock house via normal rail hoppers or move from ore bridges to self-propelled ore transfer cars, with the materials dropping into storage bins.

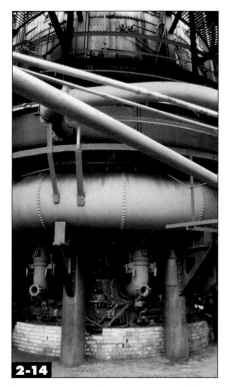

2-14

The bustle pipe and three tuyeres are visible on a preserved blast furnace at Sloss-Sheffield National Historical Site. Note the cooling lines and other details surrounding the tuyeres.

2-15

Ore piles and the high line dominate this scene at Great Lakes Steel, Detroit, in the 1940s. *Library of Congress*

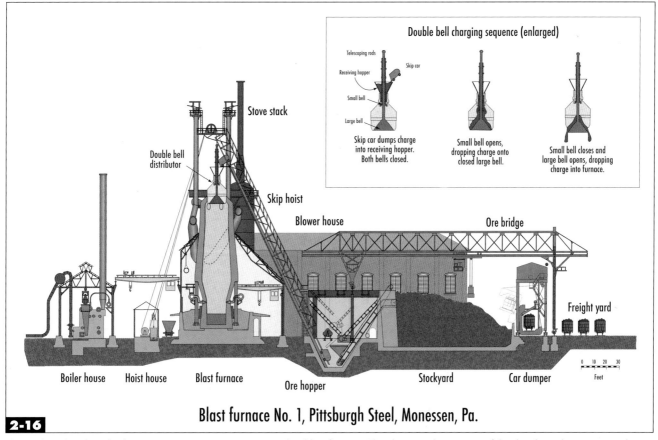

Double bell charging sequence (enlarged)

Telescoping rods

Skip car

Receiving hopper

Small bell

Large bell

Skip car dumps charge into receiving hopper. Both bells closed.

Small bell opens, dropping charge onto closed large bell.

Small bell closes and large bell opens, dropping charge into furnace.

Stove stack

Double bell distributor

Skip hoist

Blower house

Ore bridge

Freight yard

Boiler house   Hoist house   Blast furnace   Ore hopper   Stockyard   Car dumper

0 10 20 30
Feet

Blast furnace No. 1, Pittsburgh Steel, Monessen, Pa.

2-16

The stockyard and ore bridge are two common accessories with a blast furnace. This drawing shows some of the details on the apparatus that moves the raw materials from the stockyard to the furnace top. *Library of Congress, HAER*

2-17

The Chessie main line through Ashland, Ky., passes in front of the ore bridge at AK Steel.

2-18

The U.S. Steel furnace at Fairfield, Ala., is a modern design that uses conveyors to transport raw materials to the top of the furnace. Compare this to the blast furnace shown in photo 2-5 that is nearly 100 years older. *Library of Congress*

2-19

The ore distributor at the top of one furnace at Sloss-Sheffield Steel in Birmingham, Ala., is part of the double bell system. Note the access hatch, motor, and other details. *Library of Congress*

two conical bells seal in the gases and distribute the raw materials evenly around the circumference of the furnace, **2-19**. The bells operate in a sequential manner with only one open at a time so that the contents of the furnace are not open to the atmosphere (see inset in figure 2-16). Some newer furnaces do not use bells but have two or three airlock-type hoppers that discharge raw materials onto a rotating chute, which can change angles and provide more even loading.

Coke works

Coke is the most important raw material fed into the blast furnace in terms of its effect on blast furnace operation and hot metal quality. Using high-quality coke in a blast furnace results in lower coke usage, higher productivity, and lower hot metal cost. The majority of coke produced in the United States today comes from wet-charge, by-product coke oven batteries. Early coke ovens were brick domes called beehive ovens. They were frequently located near the mines where the coal came from.

The stock house operators weigh and apportion the various raw materials in a mixture designed to yield the desired hot metal and slag chemistry. The scale is either rail-mounted under the storage bins or on computer-controlled weigh hoppers that feed a conveyor belt. The weighed materials then either ride a skip car up the inclined skip hoist to the receiving hopper at the top of the furnace or travel in an automated conveyor. Large winches located in the hoist house power the cables that lift the skip cars. These are fun items to rig and animate on a blast furnace model.

A set of bins at the top of the blast furnace temporarily stores working amounts of ore, coke, and limestone. By determining a precise filling order of materials, the operators can control the gas flow and chemical reactions inside the furnace. In a bell-equipped furnace,

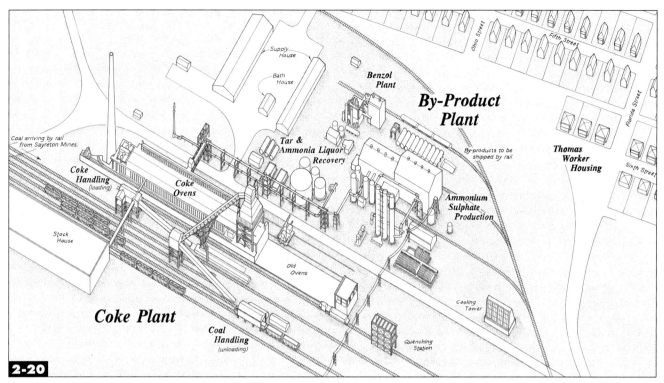

2-20

The Historic American Engineering Record documented the Thomas coke works in great detail. This view of the works shows the coke plant at the bottom left and the by-product plant at the upper center. The collection features other detailed drawings of the works and is a must for anyone considering modeling a by-product plant. *Library of Congress, HAER*

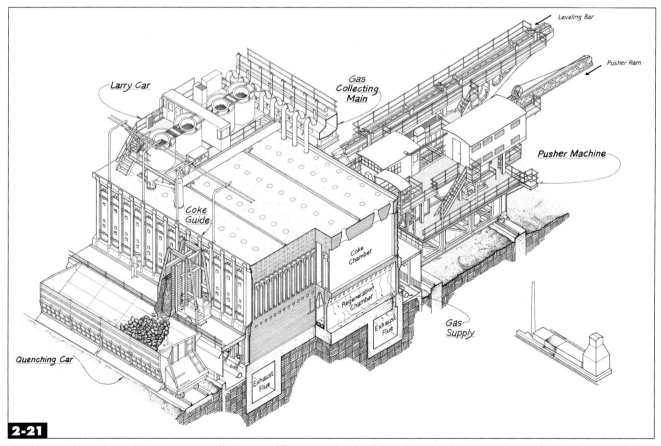

2-21

The Thomas coke works used Koppers ovens with 30 vertical flues on each side of the coking chamber. The pusher machine is a large, multiple-level device as big as a house. The larry car on the top recharges the ovens by dropping coal in the loading holes. The coke guide and quenching car reside in the foreground. *Library of Congress, HAER*

2-22

The coke batteries at Hanna furnaces at Great Lakes Steel, Detroit, had multiple pusher machines. *Library of Congress*

2-23

Incandescent coke glows cherry red as it slides through the guide car and falls into the quench car. *Library of Congress*

2-24

Gary Gealy scratchbuilt this O scale coke works. Engine 21 pulls the quenching car into position underneath the waiting door car and coke guide. The door guide will remove the door from the next oven to be pushed. It will then move the coke guide into position so that the coke pushed out of the oven will pass through it and into the waiting quenching car below. *Gary Gealy*

2-25

The coke pusher moves along the gantry tracks to position itself in front of the next oven to push. The door of the oven will be removed with the opening mechanism located on the front left corner of the coke pusher. The coke ram will then push the coke out of the oven, through the coke guide, and into the quenching car on the other side of the oven battery. *Gary Gealy*

The process of making coke in a modern facility is similar to earlier methods, except that the by-product plant captures the gases, oil, and tar driven off the coal to reuse or sell, **2-20**. A modern coke works by-product plant is a fascinating industry in its own right and makes an interesting subject to model by itself.

Instead of hemispherical beehives, modern coke ovens are vertically arranged rectangular chambers adjacent to extensive brickwork for channeling hot gases and recovering waste heat, **2-21**. The ovens form a coke battery where the individual ovens stack alongside one another like a loaf of sliced bread. A typical battery has 40 to 60 rectangular slot type ovens that share a common heating flue with the adjacent oven, **2-22**.

Coke makers use a rail-mounted larry car to place crushed coal into the chamber of an oven from above. The operators use blended coal formulas from specific mines, pulverize the coal, and sometimes add oil to get the right chemical mixture and density. The oven is heated with burning gases to about 1,900°F without letting the gas come in contact with the coal. Without oxygen to burn, the coal slowly bakes and releases most volatile matter, such as oil and tar, as vapors.

After about 18 to 24 hours, the operators remove the fresh coke from the oven. The superheated coke glows bright orange as it contacts the oxygen in the air, **2-23**. A specialized vehicle called a pusher extends a ram and pushes the incandescent coke mass from the oven through a guide car, as modeled by Gary Gealy, **2-24** and **2-25**. It falls into a waiting quench car, which moves the coke to the quench tower where a water jet sprays the coke to cool it, so it doesn't burn. It is screened and sorted into pieces ranging from 1 inch to 4 inches. The coke contains 90 to 93 percent carbon, some ash, and sulfur. The resulting lumps of coke are much stronger than the original coal and provide the energy value and free carbon needed to reduce and melt the iron ore, pellets, and sinter.

A by-product plant is essentially a chemical refinery, **2-26**. Its subsystems clean the coke-oven gas and extract many by-products from the gas. The list of chemical by-products is incredible and includes ammonia, tar, ammonium sulfate fertilizer, light oil, benzol, toluol, xylol, and naphthalene.

In 1991, *Model Railroader* magazine published a four-part series (April through October) by Dean Freytag on scratchbuilding an HO scale coke works, **2-27**. The articles take you step by step through building a coke works but without a by-product plant.

Since that time, Walthers has released a coke works kit with enhanced detail in HO and N scales. Nonetheless, the articles are worth reading even if you have the Walthers kit as they provide a lot of great ideas for detailing.

With the Walthers kit, the number of coke ovens in a single kit is probably not enough. If resources permit, adding some from additional kits will create a more realistic battery of coke ovens. The extra parts can be used to make other structures around the mill such as a

2-26

The by-product portion of the coke works is in reality a chemical refinery. This coke works is a sprawling facility along the Ohio River near Follansee, W.Va.

2-27

I scratchbuilt this N scale coke works using plans from Dean Freytag's seminal article series published in *Model Railroader* during 1991.

conveyor hoist house, stock house, and screen station.

The Walthers coke works kit does not include a by-product plant. To add a by-product plant to your coke works, you can start with a Walthers oil refinery kit. Using the HAER drawings as a guide, you can enhance the kit into a realistic model without needing to totally scratchbuild everything. The by-product plant requires rail service for shipping out the products, primarily in tank cars with some covered hoppers and boxcars.

3-1

My N scale Alkem Steel layout included a six-stack open-hearth furnace, which is a typical gabled mill structure.

Depending on the era, steelmaking in an integrated steel mill could take place in a Bessemer, basic oxygen, open-hearth, or electric arc furnace. Today, basic oxygen furnaces are the norm, having replaced open-hearth furnaces in the 1990s. Electric arc furnaces are standard at mini-mills, although some integrated facilities use them as well.

From a modeling perspective, open-hearth, basic oxygen, and electric arc furnaces appear somewhat similar as they are all housed in large, multistory, gabled, steel-frame structures, **3-1**. While these structures might appear similar, there are subtle differences that distinguish them. Unlike the blast furnace, the interior details of these structures are not readily visible and can usually be omitted without losing much visual realism.

The *USS Atlanta* was the A of the ABCD fleet built in 1882. These were the first ships for which the U.S. Navy specified open-hearth steel armor. The *Atlanta* had a thin steel hull but heavier protection in other areas. *Library of Congress*

Open-hearth steelmaking is similar to the iron puddling process (described in Chapter 1) as it uses a reverberatory-type furnace, but the process takes place at a much higher temperature. Abram Hewitt of Cooper and Hewitt, a large iron and steel works at Trenton, N.J., introduced open-hearth technology to America in 1867. However, the use of open-hearth steel technology did not spread quickly. Problems, such as firebricks being unable to withstand the intense heat of the process, held the technology back.

In 1880, less than 10 percent of American steel was produced in open-hearth furnaces. However, Bessemer steel was unable to satisfy the growing demand for high-quality steel. The uneven quality of Bessemer steel did not suit the structural steel industry. Steel with a high-tensile strength was required in applications such as bridge building, and this need spurred steelmakers to further develop the open-hearth process.

The open-hearth process could produce high-quality steel, and eventually engineers solved the technical problems encountered in the process. By 1886, open-hearth furnaces started producing steel in Cleveland, and in 1889, Pennsylvania Steel produced its first open-hearth steel.

The availability and superior strength of open-hearth steel led to its adoption as the specified material for the structural shapes and plates of U.S. Navy ships, and open-hearth steel became the preferred material for the production of ordnance, guns, armor plate, and propulsion machinery parts, **3-2**. Basic open-hearth steel overtook Bessemer production in 1908.

Open-hearth furnace

An open-hearth steel furnace was a roughly rectangular brick structure that contained a depressed, elongated, saucer-shaped floor or hearth, **3-3**. Hot gas created from burning coal, fuel oil, or natural gas passed through heat regenerators and ignited in the firebox to produce the flames needed to melt the charge, **3-4**. Workers charged the shallow refractory-lined hearth with a mixture of scrap steel and molten pig iron, **3-5**. The flames and hot gases from the firebox then passed across this charge until the temperature of the charge rose to 3,000°F, thereby melting the mixture and creating steel. As this was a reverberatory furnace, heat transferred via radiation and convection to the charge to avoid contamination with impurities in the fuel. Some open-hearth furnaces could tilt using huge hydraulic cylinders and rocker arms, but these were not as common as the stationary furnace.

Two large chambers containing a checkerwork arrangement of firebricks, through which air or gas could flow, preheated the incoming air. These

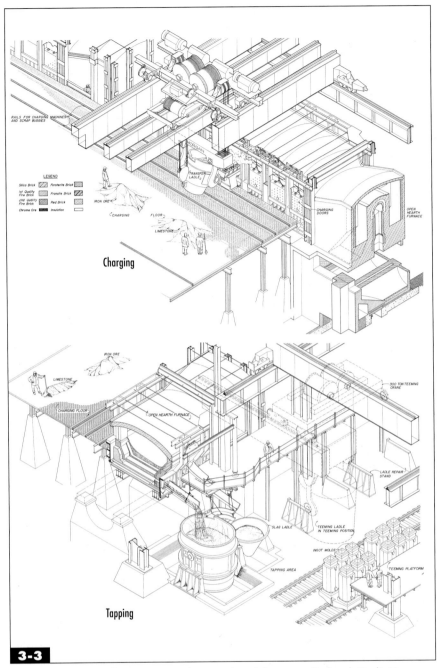

RAILS FOR CHARGING MACHINES
AND SCRAP BUGGIES

LEGEND

Silica Brick		Forsterite Brick	
1st Quality Fire Brick		Franche Brick	
2nd Quality Fire Brick		Red Brick	
Chrome Ore		Insulation	

TRANSFER
LADLE

IRON ORE

CHARGING FLOOR

LIMESTONE

CHARGING
DOORS

OPEN
HEARTH
FURNACE

Charging

IRON ORE

LIMESTONE

300 TON TEEMING
CRANE

CHARGING FLOOR

OPEN HEARTH FURNACE

LADLE REPAIR
STAND

SLAG LADLE

TEEMING LADLE
IN TEEMING POSITION

INGOT MOLDS

TAPPING AREA

TEEMING PLATFORM

Tapping

3-3

These isometric views show two areas of an open-hearth furnace at Pittsburgh Steel's Monessen works. *Library of Congress, HAER*

chambers, known as regenerators, were located at opposite ends of the furnace below the level of the hearth.

When the locomotives hauled the hot metal from the blast furnaces to the open hearth, they took it to the mixer, **3-6**. The mixer had the dual purpose of providing a supply of hot metal for the open hearths and mixing the various loads of hot metal to even out slight chemical variations. The mixer was generally a barrel-shaped, cylindrical shell lined with refractory brick having

a capacity of 800 tons or more. It sat on rockers, so operators could pour some of the contents into hot-metal ladles to charge the open hearths, **3-7**.

Because the open-hearth process took some time, six to eight hours typically, the steelmakers had the ability to adjust the raw materials during processing. They could sample the molten mixture and test it in a lab. If necessary, they could add ingredients to produce steel possessing exactly the physical and chemical properties that they desired.

The workers tapped the furnace when the heat was ready. They blew open the tapping hole with an explosive charge known as a torpedo. The molten steel flowed out of the open-hearth furnace into a hot-metal ladle. A second, smaller ladle sat alongside the hot-metal ladle to catch the slag that floated on the top of the metal. This was a sloppy process, and workers had to clean up the spilled slag and hot metal manually, a hazardous job since they had to work under the furnace. They closed the tap with a mixture of clay and dolomite in preparation for the next cast.

In most integrated mills, the open-hearth facility contained multiple furnaces usually arrayed in a line, **3-8**. Pittsburgh Steel's Monessen open hearth contained 12 separate furnaces arranged in a single structure, **3-9**. Initially built as 95-ton furnaces, they were rebuilt twice to have an ultimate capacity of 250 tons each. At 1,055 feet long and 280 feet wide, this was a huge structure. In HO scale, this building would be more than 16 feet long and 4 feet deep. Numerous tracks support the open hearth, incorporating several crossovers for operational flexibility. In most layout designs, some selective compression will be necessary to model this building.

From the outside, the open hearth looked like any generic, gable-ended mill building, except for the prominent exhaust stacks for each furnace. You can exploit this attribute to make modeling an open hearth much simpler by hiding interior details inside a metal-sided, gable-ended building built as big as the layout space can handle. A key visual element is that each furnace had its own stack. Any model of an open hearth should include one stack for each furnace. It is not necessary to model a 12-furnace works. A convincing model can be made with just four furnaces.

On the other side of the open hearths were the ingot teeming and stripping area and tracks. During the open-hearth era, molten steel usually went to rolling mills in the form of ingots.

The workers lifted the hot-metal ladle with an overhead crane and carefully teemed (poured) the steel into waiting ingot molds on specialized buggies. The ingots cooled, and when they were solid enough, the workers stripped the molds and left the glowing ingots on the buggies. Locomotives took the hot ingots to the rolling mills, soaking pits, or storage areas as needed. They also moved the slag ladle to the slag pits to be dumped.

A ladle was good for about 20 pours before it required repair, usually to the bottom stopper valve. Each ingot mold had an expected life from 6 to possibly 100 casts. The open-hearth furnace required a certain level of repair and relining after every heat. From a modeling perspective, this implies that you should have extra ladles and molds on hand at an open hearth. You should also include a ladle repair facility on the layout and feature intra-plant moves of ladles and molds from the furnaces to the repair facility in your operational scheme, **3-10**.

The mill railroad delivered scrap steel and flux material in gondolas to the stockyard. The overhead crane transferred scrap from the gondolas to smaller scrap buggies on the charging floor, which also received smaller loads of fluxing and furnace-repair materials.

In the Monessen open hearth, there were two tracks under the charging floor, one to provide coal for the gas producers and another to remove ash. Gas producers were special ovens that partially combusted coal to form a rich gaseous mixture of carbon monoxide, hydrogen, tar vapors, and other hydrocarbons that flowed through pipes into the gas main and then to the open-hearth regenerators for preheating and eventual burning. Not all open hearths used gas producers. Some relied on natural gas or fuel oil augmented with excess gas from coke ovens for fuel. In these cases, the tracks for the gas producers are not present. For example, Pittsburgh Steel removed the gas producers from Monessen in 1954 and installed fuel oil burners.

Basic oxygen furnace

In 1952, an Austrian company, Voestalpine AG, developed the first commercial basic oxygen steelmaking process. The process is called basic due to the

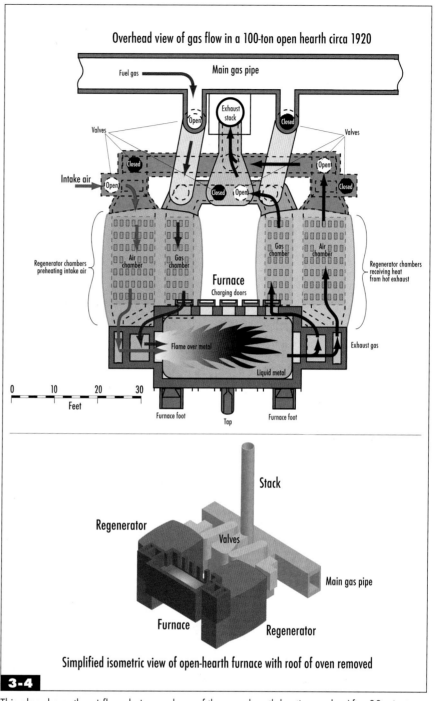

Overhead view of gas flow in a 100-ton open hearth circa 1920

Simplified isometric view of open-hearth furnace with roof of oven removed

3-4

This plan shows the airflow during a phase of the open-hearth heating cycle. After 30 minutes, the workers switch the valves to reverse the cycle. Although interesting, most of this structure is not visible inside a model open-hearth furnace.

nonacidic pH of the refractory bricks (calcium oxide and magnesium oxide) that line the vessel. The bricks wear during the heat and become part of the slag. The slag reacts to remove phosphorus and sulfur from the molten charge, which allows the refining of high-phosphorous, high-sulfur pig iron.

European companies rapidly replaced open-hearth furnaces with basic oxygen furnaces after World War II, but U.S. companies were reluctant to give up the old, tried-and-true open hearths or the last of the Bessemers. (The last U.S. Bessemer converter operated until 1968.) The first American company to use this type of furnace was McLouth Steel in Trenton, Mich., in 1954, and by 1991, all integrated mills converted to basic oxygen furnaces.

29

3-5

A worker observes as a load of molten pig iron charges an open-hearth furnace. Note the long row of ovens receding in the distance. *Library of Congress*

3-7

The crane operator pours hot metal from a ladle into the door of an open-hearth furnace. *Library of Congress*

3-6

The mixer is one of the few artifacts left from the open-hearth furnace at Tennessee Coal & Iron's Ensley works, Ensley, Ala. The open-hearth stacks still stand in the background. *Library of Congress, HAER*

Basic oxygen steelmaking is similar to the Bessemer process in that it uses high pressure flowing gas, but in this case, pure oxygen. Because pure oxygen was not available in commercial quantities during Bessemer's days, air was used as the oxidant. By using pure oxygen, the process is more efficient and scrap can be added to the charge instead of hot metal. The basic oxygen furnace consumes large amounts of oxygen. Today, a 250-ton basic oxygen furnace needs about 20 tons of pure oxygen every 40 minutes.

The physical scope of a basic oxygen furnace is immense, **3-11**. Because of the long oxygen lance and the overhead flux bin, buildings up to six stories tall house the furnace vessels. It is often the biggest building in town.

Typical dimensions for a 300-ton basic oxygen furnace vessel are 35 feet tall with an outside diameter of 26 feet. The barrel lining is 3 feet thick with a working volume of 8,000 cubic feet. Most basic oxygen furnaces have a large downcomer that emerges from the height of the roof and descends to dust catchers and other pollution-control devices, which can be a prominent modeling feature, **3-12**. A long conveyor on the exterior brings flux and additives to the overhead hoppers, **3-13**. These are the signature elements that say "basic oxygen furnace" on a large but otherwise nondescript mill structure. Adding an oxygen-producing plant to a model railroad is another signature element that suggests a basic oxygen furnace.

The operators reside in a control pulpit usually located between a pair of basic oxygen vessels. Unlike the open hearth, basic oxygen furnace operation is conducted almost in the dark with sensors and computers determining vessel inclination, additions, lance height, oxygen flow, and other control parameters.

A heat begins when the operators tilt the basic oxygen vessel about 45 degrees towards the charging aisle and dump a load of scrap from a

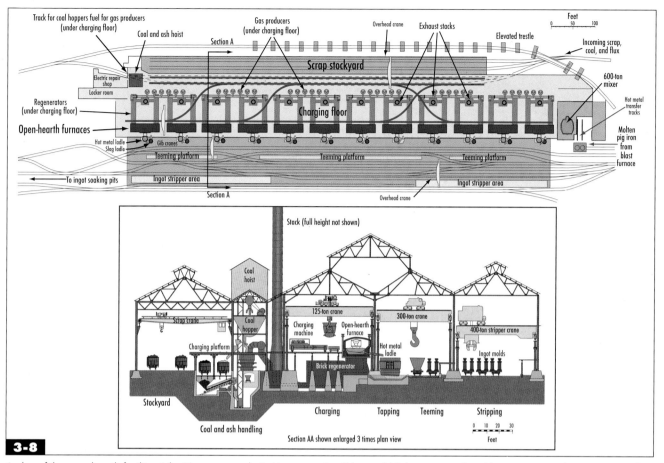

Track for coal hoppers fuel for gas producers (under charging floor)
Coal and ash hoist
Section A
Gas producers (under charging floor)
Overhead crane
Exhaust stacks
Elevated trestle
Feet
0 50 100
Incoming scrap, coal, and flux
Electric repair shop
Locker room
Scrap stockyard
600-ton mixer
Hot metal transfer tracks
Regenerators (under charging floor)
Charging floor
Molten pig iron from blast furnace
Open-hearth furnaces
Hot metal ladle
Slag ladle
Gib cranes
Teeming platform
Teeming platform
Teeming platform
To ingot soaking pits
Ingot stripper area
Ingot stripper area
Section A
Overhead crane

Stack (full height not shown)
Coal hoist
Scrap crane
Coal hopper
125-ton crane
300-ton crane
Charging machine
Open-hearth furnace
Hot metal ladle
400-ton stripper crane
Charging platform
Brick regenerator
Ingot molds
Stockyard
Coal and ash handling
Charging
Tapping
Teeming
Stripping
0 10 20 30
Feet
Section AA shown enlarged 3 times plan view

3-8

A plan of the open-hearth facility at the Monessen works in Monessen, Pa. This set of 12 furnaces used coal-burning gas producers to create the fuel used to melt and convert the iron to steel. Cross section AA is three times the scale of the plan view. The stockyard is on the left while the ingot stripping facility is on right. The long parallel gable-roof structure housing the furnaces is typical of steel mill structures.

3-9

In this aerial view of the disused Monessen steel works, the 12 stacks of the open hearth had been removed, but I retouched the photo to show where they would have been. The open hearth was immediately adjacent to the blast furnaces. In the distance, the newer basic oxygen furnace is visible. *Library of Congress, HAER*

3-10

The ladle repair facility is an interesting part of the open-hearth facility. The linings and pouring spout wear away during use and have to be repaired. *Library of Congress*

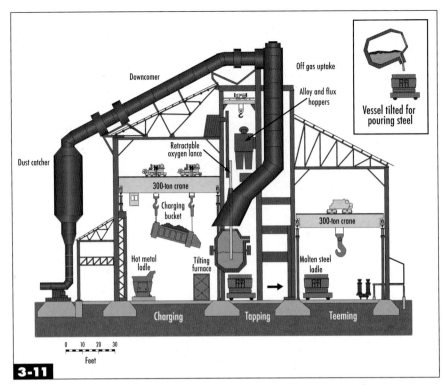

Vessel tilted for pouring steel

Off gas uptake

Downcomer

Alloy and flux hoppers

Retractable oxygen lance

Dust catcher

300-ton crane

Charging bucket

Hot metal ladle

Tilting furnace

300-ton crane

Molten steel ladle

Charging   **Tapping**   **Teeming**

0 10 20 30
Feet

3-11

The cross section shows a notional arrangement of the major components in a basic oxygen furnace. The hood has a movable collar that helps seal the vessel during oxygen blowing, which helps trap dust and waste gases.

charging box into the mouth of the cylindrical vessel, **3-14**. The scrap is about 25 to 30 percent of the heat's weight. As in the open hearth, workers use huge ladles to charge hot metal into the tilted furnace, **3-15**. This causes fumes and kish (graphite flakes from the carbon-saturated hot metal) to erupt from the vessel's mouth, where the exhaust hood captures them for emissions control. Charging takes a couple of minutes. Then the vessel is rotated back to the vertical position. Measured amounts of lime or dolomite

fluxes are automatically dropped onto the charge from overhead bins while the operator lowers the lance to a few feet above the bottom of the vessel. The flux collects the oxides, produced in the form of slag, and reduces the levels of sulfur and phosphorous in the metal. It takes approximately 730 pounds of lime to produce a ton of steel. Three hundred tons of iron is a typical charge size.

The lance is water-cooled with a multihole copper tip. The operator injects oxygen at supersonic velocities to start the reactions. To minimize the introduction

of contaminants, the oxygen is 99.5 to 99.8 percent pure. Some basic oxygen furnaces insert the oxygen from below, but the process is similar.

Blowing continues for a predetermined time, typically 15 to 20 minutes, and the lance is generally preprogrammed to move to different heights during the blowing period.

At this point, the lance is raised and the vessel tilted toward the charging aisle for sampling and temperature tests. The computer controller adds flux and bulk alloys from overhead bins into the ladle. A whole sub-industry exists to supply these additives. Some of their facilities resemble steel mini-mills and would make interesting subjects for a model railroad side industry.

The basic oxygen process can convert a 300-ton charge to steel in approximately 45 minutes, of which half that time is active blowing. The basic oxygen process increased productivity, so generally, two basic oxygen furnaces could replace a dozen open-hearth furnaces. The basic oxygen process predated continuous casting, and the first basic oxygen furnaces were frequently built in converted open-hearth buildings. As a consequence, ladle sizes remained unchanged in the renovated open-hearth shops, and ingot-pouring aisles were built in the new shops, **3-16**.

Once the heat is ready for tapping, workers position a preheated ladle on a carrier car under the furnace vessel. They move the vessel towards the tapping aisle, and steel emerges from the taphole in the upper cone section of

3-12

Ken McCorry's basic oxygen furnace occupies a corner of his huge HO scale layout. The downcomer descending from the roof is a clear telltale that this is a basic oxygen furnace.

3-13

The long conveyor on the outside of the basic oxygen furnace at Wheeling Steel transports flux and alloy materials to the hoppers above the basic oxygen furnace vessel.

3-14

Wheeled carriers are becoming more prevalent on steel mills as they replace railcars. Here a wheel carrier charges a basic oxygen furnace with scrap. *Library of Congress*

3-15

Hot metal charges a basic oxygen furnace at Geneva Steel in Utah. *Mark Hemphill*

3-16

Ingot molds on buggies wait their turn for teeming at Republic Steel in Cleveland in 1979. Note the basic oxygen furnace in the background, a sign that this was an early implementation of basic oxygen technology, as continuous casting has not yet replaced ingot molding. At this time, Republic Steel operated both open-hearth and basic oxygen furnaces at the mill. *Library of Congress, HAER*

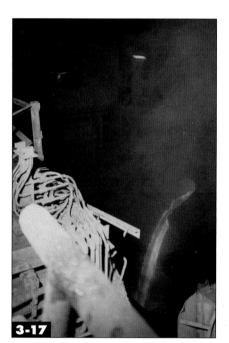

3-17

Slag flowing out of a basic oxygen furnace drops into a slag ladle at U.S. Steel's Homestead works. Slag has many industrial uses including cinder blocks, road fill, sandblasting grit, and railroad ballast. *Library of Congress*

the vessel. The taphole is generally plugged with material that prevents slag from leaving as the vessel turns down, but when steel touches the plug material, it burns through immediately, allowing the steel to pour.

To minimize slag entering the ladle at the end of tapping, various slag stoppers have been designed, but it is up to the operator to properly position and engage them, one of the few non-automated tasks in the overall process. They try to avoid getting slag in the

hot-metal ladle because that can allow phosphorus to reenter the steel. Ladle additives are available to manipulate some impurities, but nothing can be done to alter the phosphorus if it reenters the steel.

After pouring steel into the ladle, the operators turn the vessel upside down and tap the remaining slag into the slag pot, **3-17**. With the vessel back in an upright position many shops blow residual slag with nitrogen to coat the inside of the vessel with a thin layer of

slag. This process is known as slag splashing. The slag coats the refractory, cools, solidifies, and creates a solid layer of slag that serves as a consumable refractory layer. This slag layer decreases the wear rate of the vessel's refractory, increases lining life, and decreases operating costs. Sometimes repairing high-wear areas in the vessel with refractory materials may be necessary. Once vessel maintenance is complete, the vessel is ready to receive the next charge.

3-18

The pollution-control features of this basic oxygen furnace are quite evident and present both a modeling challenge and the opportunity to make an impressive model.

3-19

The Dorr thickener (left) is part of the pollution-control system at Weirton Steel. It cleans water by settling out the particulates. The environmental covers on the uptakes and downcomer of the basic oxygen furnace are also very prominent features.

A water-cooled hood serves as the primary gas-handling system in most basic oxygen furnaces. The hood has heat exchangers to generate steam for the rest of the mill by using waste heat from the exhaust. Many of the hoods have open combustion designs in which excess air injected at the mouth of the hood completely burns the carbon monoxide. The gases are then cooled and cleaned either in a wet scrubber or in a dry electrostatic precipitator. Another gas-handling system suppresses combustion and handles gases in an unburned state. The gases are cleaned in a wet scrubber before being ignited prior to discharge. In both cases, the cleaned gases must meet government-mandated levels for particulate matter. It's hard to differentiate the two systems in a model railroad, but it is an area a modeler can research further if desired.

Secondary emissions, those associated with charging and tapping the basic oxygen furnace vessel, or emissions escaping the main hood during oxygen blowing may be captured by exhaust systems through local hoods or high-canopy hoods located in the trusses of the shop. Typically, a fabric collector or bag house collects these fugitive emissions. Bag houses are usually located around the outside of basic oxygen furnaces and make an interesting detail to add to a model, **3-18**.

The particulate matter captured in the primary system, whether in the form of sludge from wet scrubbers or dry dust from precipitators, must be processed before recycling. Sludge from wet scrubbers requires an extra drying step. You should attempt to simulate the sludge recovery system, with Dorr thickeners or settling tanks,

in a basic oxygen furnace model and other steel mills, **3-19**.

After it is removed from the steel-making furnace, steel often undergoes additional refining in transport vessels, smaller furnaces, or a ladle. This refining can have several purposes, such as degassing (the removal of oxygen, sulfur, hydrogen, and other gases by exposing the steel to a low-pressure environment); removing carbon monoxide through deoxidizers such as aluminum, titanium, and silicon; and changing the composition of irremovable substances, such as oxides, to further improve mechanical properties.

The basic oxygen furnace has transformed the steel industry since World War II, **3-20**. Although it was not recognized at the time, the process made it possible to couple melting with continuous casting. The continuous caster results in improved hot metal quality and productivity. The basic oxygen process is today's dominant steelmaking technology, producing 60 percent of the world's total output of crude steel.

Electric arc furnace

The final common method of making steel is with an electric arc furnace, **3-21**. In an electric arc furnace, electric

3-20

The basic oxygen furnace, typified by this example at Severstal Steel (formerly Rouge Steel) in Dearborn, Mich., transformed steelmaking. Here, the basic oxygen furnace is undergoing repairs.

current forms arcs between two or three carbon electrodes. Electric arc furnaces require a power source to supply the charge necessary to generate the electric arc, and they typically use electricity purchased from an outside source. Electric arc furnaces primarily use scrap metal for their iron source, which means that it takes less energy to melt the iron per ton produced.

An electric arc furnace is now almost synonymous with a steel mini-mill, although some integrated steel mills have electric arc furnaces as well as basic oxygen furnaces. Mini-mills melt recycled ferrous scrap in electric arc furnaces to make a limited quantity of steel products including carbon steel bars, rebar, wire rods, and light to medium structural items for the construction industry.

The first electric arc furnaces were developed in France during the early 1900s. Early electric arc furnaces were used sparingly in general steel production, being used mostly for specialty steels such as alloy steel for machine tools and spring steel. By 1920, electric arc furnaces were common but only produced about 3 percent of U. S. steel. While electric arc furnaces were widely used in World War II for production of alloy steels, **3-22**, it was only later that electric steelmaking began to expand.

Having a low capital cost, mini-mills were quickly established in postwar Europe. The mini-mill concept got started in the United States in 1969 when Nucor built one in Darlington, S.C., and other manufacturers soon followed. They are typically located close to their customers as well as near sources of scrap. By being able to start and stop quickly, electric arc furnaces allow steel mills to vary production according to demand. In addition to their low capital cost, mini-mills have a cost advantage in labor as well. However, mini-mills are very sensitive to scrap prices, and when scrap prices rise, they can lose their cost advantage over integrated mills.

The low overall cost also allows them to successfully compete with larger steelmakers for carbon steel long products: structural steel, rod and bar,

3-21

An electric arc casts a yellow glow in the shop and creates an ear-splitting din as it refines steel at Steel of West Virginia in 1997.

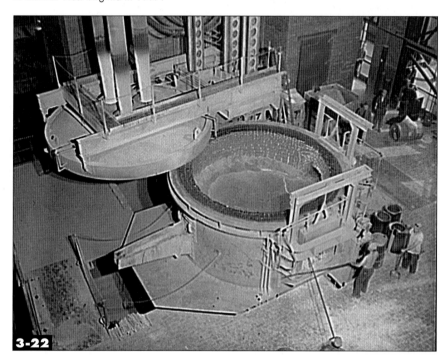

3-22

Refined alloy steel in the electric arc furnace is ready for ingot casting in this 1940s photograph. The slag layer on top of the molten steel prevents the hot steel from oxidizing, which preserves its high quality. Steel will be drawn off through the spout at the left into ladles in the pit at Allegheny Ludlum Steel, Brackenridge, Pa. *Library of Congress*

wire, and fasteners. Mini-mills also produce merchant products such as angles, flats, and merchant bar, which they sell to fabricators. The more demanding flat products, such as sheet steel and heavy steel plate, still require using blast furnaces and basic oxygen furnaces, although some mini-mills are beginning to enter this business.

Mini-mills vary in size from single-plant operations with an annual capacity of 150,000 tons to multi-plant companies with capacities of up to 2 million tons per year. More than 100 mini-mills operate in 27 different states and account for about 38 percent of total U.S. steel industry shipments. This pattern also applies globally, and there

White-hot specialty steel pours like water from a 35-ton electric furnace at Allegheny Ludlum Steel, Brackenridge, Pa., in 1941. The furnace is tilted for the pouring, and flying sparks accompany the flowing liquid steel. *Library of Congress*

A CROW SW1001 pulls a cut of flatcars around the perimeter of one of the mills at the Mittal Steel Cleveland works in 2008. The huge scrap piles have been sorted and wait to be melted in the basic oxygen furnace in the background. *Thomas Habak*

This American Steel Foundries (now ASF-Keystone) mill in Granite City, Ill., produces trucks for freight cars. A few freight cars arrive inbound, but all finished product is trucked out. Quite a bit of intra-plant switching takes place here. *Mike Mautner*

Mini-mills and basic oxygen furnaces depend on a steady supply of scrap. This scrap processor is using a magnet to load shredded scrap into charging buckets in South Chicago in February 2007. *Joel Hinkhouse*

are mini-mills in nearly every country. Some of the larger mini-mills have expanded their production capabilities to make large structural shapes and have driven some integrated producers out of this market.

An electric arc furnace consists of a refractory-lined vessel, usually water-cooled in larger sizes, covered with a retractable roof, through which two or three graphite electrodes enter the furnace. The furnace is composed of three sections: the shell, which consists of the sidewalls and a lower steel bowl; the hearth, which consists of the refractory that lines the lower bowl; and the roof, which may be refractory-lined or water-cooled, and can be shaped as a section of a sphere or as a conic section.

The hearth is usually hemispherical in shape. The furnace is generally raised off the ground floor so that ladles and slag pots can easily be maneuvered under either end of the furnace. Separate from the furnace structure are the electrode supports, electrical system, and tilting platform on which the furnace rests. Two configurations are possible: either the electrode supports and the roof tilt with the furnace, or they are fixed to the raised platform.

The electric arc furnace operates as a batch melting process, producing molten steel in successive heats, **3-23**. The operating cycle is called the tap-to-tap cycle and is made up of the following operations: furnace charging, melting, refining, and resetting.

The tap-to-tap time can range from 35 to 60 minutes.

Before charging the furnace, the operators carefully select the grade of steel to be made. The scrapyard operator prepares buckets of scrap according to the needs of the melter, **3-24**. The composition of the scrap charge is important to ensure proper melt chemistry and good melting conditions. The scrap must be layered in the bucket according to size and density to promote the rapid formation of a liquid pool of steel in the hearth while providing protection for the sidewalls and roof from electric arc radiation. The charge can include lime and carbon, or these elements can be injected into the furnace during the heat.

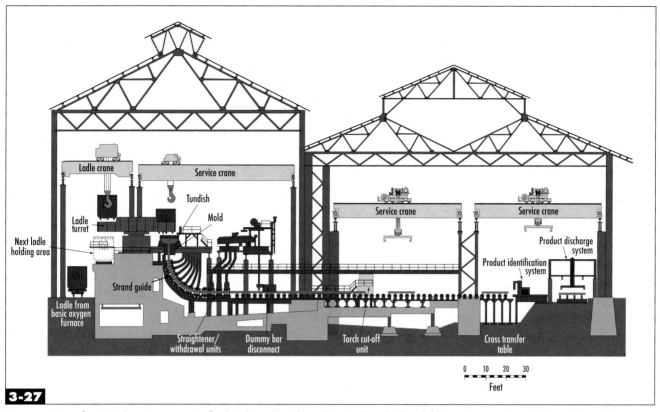

Ladle crane

Service crane

Tundish

Ladle turret

Mold

Next ladle holding area

Service crane

Service crane

Product discharge system

Product identification system

Strand guide

Ladle from basic oxygen furnace

Straightener/ withdrawal units

Dummy bar disconnect

Torch cut-off unit

Cross transfer table

0 10 20 30
Feet

3-27

A cross section of a typical continuous caster facility shows how the molten steel gradually solidifies as it moves through the mold, straightener, cutting, and product discharge process.

When the scrap is ready, the operators raise the roof with the electrodes, and it swings off to the side of the furnace. They charge the furnace with scrap from a bottom-drop bucket, and the roof swings back over the furnace. The electrodes are lowered and strike an arc on the scrap, which starts the melting portion of the cycle. If the electrodes are aligned so that the current passes above the metal, the metal is heated by radiation from the arc. If the electrodes are aligned so that the current passes through the metal, the resistance of the current generates heat as well as the arc radiation.

The number of charge buckets of scrap required to produce a heat of steel is dependent on the volume of the furnace and the scrap density. Two or three are typical although some operations achieve a single bucket charge. In some electric arc furnaces, continuous charging operations eliminate the charging cycle.

The melting period is the heart of electric arc furnace operations. Electrical energy is supplied via the graphite electrodes. Initially, the operator uses an intermediate voltage tap until the electrodes bore into the scrap. After a few minutes, the electrodes will have penetrated the scrap sufficiently so that a high voltage can create a long arc without fear of radiation damage to the roof. The long arc maximizes the transfer of power to the scrap, and a liquid pool of metal will form in the furnace hearth. As the melting starts, the arc is erratic and unstable. As the furnace atmosphere heats up, the arc stabilizes, and once the molten pool is formed, the arc becomes quite stable and the average power input increases.

Once a molten pool of steel exists in the furnace, operators can inject oxygen directly into the bath. This oxygen will react with components in the bath, and as in a basic oxygen furnace, these reactions generate heat and supply additional energy that aids in the melting of the scrap. The metallic oxides that form end up in the slag.

Refining operations in the electric arc furnace remove phosphorus, sulfur, aluminum, silicon, manganese, and carbon from the steel and dissolved gases such as hydrogen and nitrogen.

Oxygen is blown into the bath to lower the carbon content to the desired level for tapping.

Once the desired steel composition and temperature are achieved in the furnace, workers open the taphole, tilt the furnace, and pour the steel into a ladle for transfer to the next batch operation. During the tapping process, they may add bulk alloys based on the bath analysis and the desired steel grade. Deoxidizers may be added to the steel to lower the oxygen content prior to further processing. This is commonly referred to as "blocking the heat" or "killing the steel."

Furnace turnaround is the period following completion of tapping until recharging for the next heat. During this time, an operator raises the electrodes and the roof and inspects the furnace lining refractory for damage and repairs it if necessary.

Mini-mills are ideal subjects for a model railroad where space is at a premium. As in most steel mill structures, the exterior of the structure is a series of gable-end steel sheds. Usually the electric furnace is hidden inside the

3-28 This photo shows rolling mills in action. Since this complex machinery is largely hidden inside the rolling mill structures on a model railroad, it can be omitted if desired. *Siemens AG*

3-29 The continuous caster is several stories tall. The tundish is the drum-like object in the center, and the strand guide arcs below it. *Library of Congress*

structure with roof top vents and perhaps a downcomer as the only visible clues. The electrodes are one of the most important elements in the electric arc steelmaking process, and having spare electrodes around is a key detail when modeling an electric arc furnace. The mill receives carloads of scrap, covered hoppers of flux, and boxcars with sundry supplies, **3-25**. They ship out finished products in coil cars, boxcars, or flatcars.

Steel scrap

Because of the importance of scrap in steelmaking, of all the world's industries, the steel industry is probably the biggest user of recycled materials by ton, **3-26**. Steel scrap is available in many forms including home, prompt, and obsolete or post-consumer scrap. Home scrap is generated in the plant by the steelmaking and shaping processes. With the advent of continuous casting, the quantity of home scrap has diminished, and it is now necessary for integrated mills to buy scrap on the market. Prompt scrap is scrap generated during the manufacturing of steel products, and it finds its way into the recycling stream very quickly. Many steel mills have agreements with manufacturers to buy their prompt

scrap. Obsolete or post-consumer scrap returns to the market after a product has ended its useful life. Cans return to the mill very quickly, but autos have an average life of 12 years.

Scrap comes in a variety of sizes, prices, and chemical makeup—all of which makes the purchase and melting of scrap a very complex issue. Very large pieces of scrap can be difficult to melt and may damage the vessel when charged. Some scrap may contain oil or surface oxidation. Obsolete scrap may contain hazardous or explosive objects.

Selecting scrap is further complicated by the wide variety of steel products that the mill may produce. Deep-drawing steels used in automobile body panels limit the maximum residual amount of copper, tin, nickel, chromium, and molybdenum content to less than 0.13 percent, while other products allow this amount to range as high as 0.80 percent. Since these elements cannot be oxidized from the steel, their content in the final product can only be reduced by dilution with very high-purity scrap or hot metal. This use of pure hot metal in the basic oxygen furnace to dilute contamination is one advantage basic oxygen steelmaking has over electric arc steelmaking.

Shaping steel

Integrated mills use two primary methods to shape molten steel into a solid form for use at finishing mills: ingot casting and continuous casting. Ingot casting is the traditional method in which the molten metal is poured into ingot molds and allowed to cool and solidify. However, continuous casting became common in the 1980s and currently accounts for almost 100 percent of forming operations. Continuous casting, in which the steel is cast directly into a moving mold, reduces the loss of steel during processing and saves on the energy required for reheating.

Ingot casting

In this forming method, casters pour, or teem, molten steel from refractory-lined ladles into a series of ingot molds. After the ingots solidify, the molds are stripped and placed in soaking pits to equalize the internal and external temperature. Following the soak, the ingots are moved to large primary rolling mills and hot rolled to produce slabs, blooms, or billets depending on the desired products. Ingots range in size from several hundred pounds for specialty steels to 300 tons for large forging applications.

Primary rolling mills, also called blooming mills or slabbing mills, consist of a number of rolling stands that shape the hot steel into the desired semi-finished shape. As an ingot moves through the stands, it is gradually squeezed between the heavy rolls.

Billets have cast section sizes up to about 7" square, and bloom sections range from approximately 7" square to about 15" by 23". Slab castings range in thickness from 2" to 16" and can be more than 100" wide.

To make billets, the rollers first shape the steel into blooms, and then the steel goes through another set of rolls in a billet mill. Each time the ingot goes through the rolls, it is further reduced in one dimension. Blooming mills are either two-high or three-high, depending on the number of rolls used. The two rolls of the two-high mill can be reversed so that the ingot is flattened and lengthened as it passes back and forth between the rolls. The top and bottom rolls of the three-high mill turn in one direction while the middle roll turns in the opposite direction. The bottom and middle rolls flatten the ingot, and it ends up on a runout table. The table rises, and the steel feeds through the top and middle rolls. Finally, the continuous (or cross-country) mill is a third type of blooming mill. This mill has a series of two-high rolls. As many as 15 passes may be required to reduce an ingot 21" square in cross section to a bloom 8" square in cross section. Most of the rolls used in these mills are horizontal, but there are also vertical rolls that squeeze the blooms or slabs from the sides.

The hot sections of steel move from one station to another on a series of roller conveyors. Shears cut the uneven ends off and then cut the single long piece into shorter lengths. The sheared-off ends go to the scrap line. High-pressure water jets remove mill scale that forms on the surface of the slabs. An oxygen flame burns off, or scarfs, surface defects on the finished blooms and slabs.

The slabs, blooms, and billets then go to finishing mills where they are formed

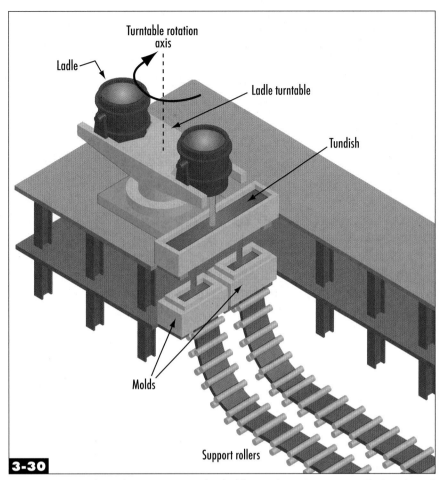

An isometric view shows the arrangement of a double-strand continuous caster. The liquid metal partially cools in the tundish before entering the support rollers.

Water sprays cool slabs as they pass through a six-stand finishing mill at Republic Steel in 1941. *Library of Congress*

3-32

A torch unit cuts a slab. Modeling the glowing slabs could be achieved by lighting tinted acrylic plastic pieces. *Siemens AG*

3-33

Spare parts and assorted junk clutters the ground around the blast furnace at Weirton Steel. Clutter like this is found around many parts of a facility including rolling mills. Identification codes can be seen on the ends of the steel slabs stacked in the foreground.

into special shapes and forms such as bars, beams, plates, and sheets. The steel is still not completely finished, but it is closer to the form in which it will eventually be used in manufactured goods. Blooms and billets become rails, wire rods, wires, bars, tubes, seamless pipe, and I- and H-beams. Slabs become plates, sheets, strips, or welded pipe.

After they are hot rolled, steel plates or shapes undergo further chemical processing, such as cleaning and pickling, to remove surface oxides; cold rolling to improve strength and surface finish; annealing (stress relieving); and galvanizing or aluminizing for corrosion resistance.

Continuous casting

Continuous or strand casting eliminates the need to produce ingots and the use of soaking pits, **3-27**. With the introduction of continuous casting in the 1950s, ingot casting was gradually phased out. In addition to costing less, continuously cast steels have more uniform compositions and properties than ingot-cast steels. Continuous casting produces an endless length of steel that is cut into long slabs or blooms ready for shaping in rolling mills, **3-28**.

Locomotives or wheeled carriers transport ladles of liquid steel from the electric arc furnace or basic oxygen furnace to the continuous casting

machine. An overhead crane raises the ladle onto a turret that rotates the ladle into the casting position above the tundish. Operators place a steel dummy bar in the hole in the mold's bottom to prevent liquid steel from flowing out of the mold. They pour the steel into the tundish, **3-29**. It flows into the water-cooled copper mold and adheres to the dummy bar. The steel in the mold partially solidifies, producing a steel strand with a solid outer shell and a liquid core, **3-30**. Once the steel shell has a sufficient thickness, the machine grabs the dummy bar and proceeds to withdraw the partially solidified strand out of the mold along with the dummy bar. The liquid steel continues to pour into the mold to replenish the withdrawn steel at an equal rate.

Upon exiting the mold, the strand is sprayed with water to cool and further solidify it, **3-31**. Once the strand is fully solidified—but still red hot—a machine removes the dummy bar and sets it aside for reuse. The strand proceeds through the straightener, a device that trues up the shape. It then passes through a torch-cutting station that cuts it into individual pieces, **3-32**, and then it proceeds to other rolling stations for any final shaping and treating.

The machinery that rolls, shapes, pickles, and heat-treats steel is too

valuable to leave exposed to the elements. The slabs of steel undergoing shaping must also be protected from rain and snow. Thus, the shaping process largely takes place inside covered buildings. As in the case of open-hearth furnaces and electric arc furnaces, rolling mills can be modeled with the ubiquitous gable-end steel sheds embellished with stacks, piping, and pollution-control equipment as you see fit, using prototype photos as a guide.

Detailing the inside of these structures is a challenging modeling job. A few model-kit companies produce rolling mill stand kits, but this just scratches the surface of what is needed. Instead of detailing the complete interior, a possible compromise is to open a door on the side or end of a plain rolling mill structure and place just enough of the machinery inside to give a hint of the interior. Adding a few flashing orange lights helps create the illusion that red-hot steel is being squeezed, pressed, and drawn inside.

Many mills employ large yards to store finished slabs. Often, the slabs have identification codes spray-painted on their ends. The rail yards and areas surrounding rolling mills should be sprinkled liberally with slabs and extra parts for the machinery inside to simulate normal clutter, **3-33**.

Railroads and transportation

4-1

The early history of steel and railroads in the United States is inextricably intertwined. Bessemer steel rails had a stimulating effect on the railroad industry and its westward expansion. The first steel rails used in the United States were imported, and they were expensive. Thus, railroads used them sparingly in areas where the traffic justified it. (The British were the first to discover Bessemer steel's superior durability and use it in rails.)

In 1870, there were three Bessemer mills operating, with the number growing to 11 by 1876 and 24 by 1880. By 1880, U.S. steel rail overtook imported rail. Several railroads, such as Pennsylvania Railroad, started their own steel mills to ensure a supply of rail. American steel and railroad companies and their executives were closely linked. For example, Andrew Carnegie served 12 years with the Pennsylvania Railroad before building his steel empire.

A PLW SC15A pushes a cut of flatcars at ArcelorMittal's East Chicago plant in March 2001.
Joel Hinkhouse

FOUR

41

4-2

A common carrier such as B&O supplies raw materials to steel mills. Here, B&O 5964 and 6506 switch in the shadow of the Republic Steel mill in Youngstown, Ohio, in May 1977. *Roger Durfree*

4-3

The Weirton Steel Railroad maintained a diesel engine service facility at the Walnut Street Yard with a sanding tower (at right) and fuel facilities. Note the junk slag pots in the background at left.

led to bigger locomotives and heavier cars, which, in turn, required still heavier rail.

As steel mills became integrated, their railroads became an important component, **4-1**. As part of his complete integration of the steel industry, Andrew Carnegie founded the Pittsburgh, Bessemer & Lake Erie Railroad in 1897 to haul iron ore from the port at Conneaut, Ohio, to Carnegie Steel plants in Pittsburgh and the surrounding area. To maintain profitability, the railroad back-hauled coal north to the lakes for shipping on the bulk carriers that Carnegie also owned. Carnegie merged a group of smaller railroads including the Pittsburgh, Shenango & Lake Erie and the Butler & Pittsburgh Railroad to form the PB&LE. It was renamed the Bessemer & Lake Erie Railroad in 1900 under an exclusive 999-year lease to Carnegie Steel and then to U.S. Steel when it acquired Carnegie Steel in 1901. The B&LE changed hands in the 1980s and eventually became part of Canadian National in 2004.

The Union Railroad founded in 1896 is another important steel-hauling railroad that also served the Pittsburgh region. Through leases and mergers, it acquired 65 miles of mainline track and approximately 200 miles of yard track and sidings. The railroad achieved a peak tonnage in 1951 of 74.5 million net tons of revenue freight. It is still in action as part of the Transtar System.

Other well-known steel-hauling railroads include the Delray Connecting Railroad near Detroit, the Elgin, Joliet & Eastern Railway that served Chicago area steel mills, and the Philadelphia Bethlehem & New England, a captive railroad of Bethlehem Steel. There were many other steel-hauling railroads, usually Class III and captive to their mill. Some like the EJ&E had a broader scope and served nonsteel industries in urban areas, while others, such as the Aliquippa & Ohio River Railroad, outlived the steel mills they were founded to serve.

I will focus on the captive steel mill railroads and the specialized equipment that they used in the steel industry. Most steel mills had yards or

The advantages of steel rail over iron rail resulted from different means of manufacture. Early iron rail was made from wrought iron instead of cast iron because the shock and stress of wheels rolling on the rail would fracture the brittle cast iron. The puddling process used in making wrought iron limited production to small iron rods, which the puddlers had to bundle and roll into rails. Once in place, the pressure and pounding of the railroad wheels tended to break the rails into the individual rods. Steel rails did not have these vulnerable layers as one rail came from a single ingot that rollers

squeezed into its final shape. Steel rails would wear away before delaminating but only after many more ton-miles passed over them. Early steel was expensive, so railroads limited their use of it.

A turning point occurred in 1883, when the cost of steel rails fell below that of iron. By 1890, the majority of all new railroad mileage in the United States was laid with steel rails. Use of steel rail allowed railroads to increase traffic density and run heavier trains at higher speeds without excessive rail wear and risk of fracture. In a sense, a vicious cycle emerged as stronger rail

access to yards where interchange with common-carrier railroads took place, **4-2**. To illustrate how a captive mill railroad served its mill and interchanged with Class I haulers, let's take an in-depth look at the Weirton Steel Railroad, **4-3**, a typical integrated steel mill railroad.

The railroad served Weirton Steel in Weirton, W.Va., about 37 miles west of Pittsburgh. The steel mill got its start when Ernest Weir built a sheet and tinplate mill on the Ohio River, **4-4**. The company grew and developed other factories, mostly making tinplate, in West Virginia and Ohio. In 1929, a merger created National Steel, with Weirton Steel as its major division. Utilizing its tinplate capacity, Weirton specialized in the beverage can market, becoming "the home of the mighty tin can." In the late 1960s and early 1970s, National Steel modernized Weirton Steel by adding a basic oxygen furnace, a continuous caster, and a new coke plant. In the 1980s, Weirton suffered from the downturn in the U.S. steel market, and its steel shipments peaked in 1984 at 2.1 million tons.

Weirton's hot metal facilities included four blast furnaces capable of producing approximately 2.5 million net tons of hot metal per year. The steel-producing shop included two-vessel basic oxygen furnaces with two ladle treatment stations, two vacuum degassing facilities, and a 48" four-strand continuous caster capable of producing approximately 3 million tons of raw steel per year.

Weirton was capable of producing hot-rolled sheet, cold-rolled sheet, galvanized, electro-galvanized, and tinplate products for use in construction and container manufacturing. Finishing facilities included a 54" hot strip mill, 54" and 48" continuous picklers, two 48" five-stand and one 48" four-stand tandem cold mills, batch anneal, three continuous anneal lines, three temper mills (48" one-stand for sheet products, a 40" two-stand, and 45" two-stand for tin products), two double cold reducing mills, two 48" and one 42" hot-dip galvanizing lines, one 38" electro-galvanizing line, and four tinplate lines.

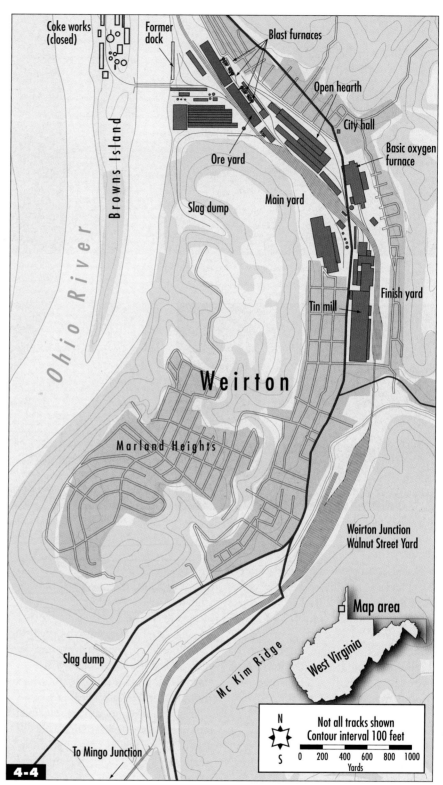

4-4

Weirton Steel in Weirton, W.Va., was founded along the Ohio River. It grew to include blast furnaces, open-hearth furnaces, and basic oxygen furnaces.

The plant was successful for about 20 years under employee ownership until 2003 when it filed for bankruptcy. A series of mergers and sell-offs occurred with ArcelorMittal eventually taking over. The company permanently idled the hot end between 2005 and 2007, while keeping some of the tin mill operational using steel from some of its other lower cost mills. Weirton's blast furnaces, basic oxygen furnace, and support structures were torn down in 2007.

4-5

C&O 2-6-4 K-4 Kanawha Locomotive passes Armco Steel (now AK Steel) in Ashland, Ky. *C&O Historical Society*

4-6

Weirton Steel used the former PRR station as a storage building.

4-7

The former open-hearth structure became a slag dump.

4-8

Some of the Weirton Steel locomotive fleet waits in the Walnut Street Yard. Note the ballast maintenance cars in the background.

In addition to its railroad, Weirton Steel had one of the largest docks on the Ohio River. Built in the 1950s, the harbor and dock provided facilities for loading finished steel and unloading scrap metal from barges. But by the 1980s, nearly all of Weirton Steel's raw materials used in the steelmaking process were delivered by rail.

Weirton was a favorite of railfans because an elevated, public road ran through the mill, which made taking photos easy, and for its widespread use of Alco locomotives.

In its heyday during in the 1980s, the Weirton Steel railroad plant had 27 Alco locomotives that performed all the switching for the large integrated mill. Weirton Steel had a long history of ordering Alcos as far back as the steam days when Alco 0-4-0s to 0-8-0s were used for switching chores. The first Alco diesels, an S1 and two

S2s, arrived in 1945, and in 1952, more diesels replaced the steamers. Between 1958 and 1970, Weirton acquired 12 more S2s and an S4. They also converted a derelict locomotive into a slug (numbered 100) for use in the ore yard. A slug is a locomotive with traction motors but no prime mover or engine. It utilizes electrical power from the mother engine via multiple unit connections. Slugs are especially useful in slow, heavy drags like those usually encountered in steel mill transfer runs.

Weirton Steel had more than 700 railroad cars of its own for use in the mill. These included 170 flatcars for hauling coil steel within the plant, 150 40- and 50-foot gondolas for general use, 100 hopper cars, 130 hot cars (35-foot flatcars for hot steel slabs), 20 hot metal cars, 100 cinder pots or slag cars, and 2 ore transfer cars with drop

bottoms. The hot metal cars were 55-foot submarine, or bottle-type cars, with a 380-ton capacity riding on four 4-wheel trucks. Three cabooses, for use on the slag runs, were homebuilt and numbered 1, 2, and 3. Two were cut-down boxcars; the other resembled a Bessemer & Lake Erie caboose.

Because Weirton Steel depended on its railroad, it had a fully equipped shop to keep things running smoothly and safely. The shop could do routine maintenance as well as complete overhauls, except for electrical work. Over the years, the railroad modified its Alco locomotives with new turbochargers, replacement trucks, increased engine horsepower, and remote control. The remote units allowed operation by two-man crews in hazardous operations like hot-metal pours. Weirton also had a five-man track gang and a car-shop crew.

An SW1500 backs away after spotting a hot metal submarine car under the spout at the northern blast furnace at Weirton Steel.

With the locomotive safely out of the way, hot metal flows into a bottle car on the east side of the blast furnace while...

In operations prior to 1980, Weirton received cars in interchange from Conrail. This was the normal mode of operation for mill switchers. Class I or II railroads brought in outside cars and dropped them off at an interchange yard that could belong either to the mill or to the mainline railroad. The mill switchers dropped off outbound cars and picked up inbound cars. How the cars were arranged in these trains, whether they were classified or not, depended on the arrangement the two railroads had with each other. Some interchange yards were alongside the Class I main lines with their resulting parade of nonsteel related trains, such as Armco Steel (now AK) in Ashland, Ky., the C&O, PRR lines through Pittsburgh, the D&RGW, and the UP, 4-5. Others, such as Weirton Steel, Bethlehem Steel Sparrows Point, and U.S. Steel on Zug Island, Mich., were on a branch line, or at the end of one, built primarily to serve that industry.

In July 1980, Conrail and Weirton signed an agreement for the steel company to lease Conrail's 33-track, 1,100-car capacity Weirton Junction Yard (renamed Walnut Street Yard) and three miles of track that bisected the plant. The Weirton railroad expanded to become a "real railroad" as opposed to just a captive mill switcher.

The railroad had 125 track-miles spread across four yards and two mains. Within the mill, there were three yards: the main yard, an ore yard, and a finish

...slag fills the cinder car on west side. Old parts and used equipment lay near the tracks.

yard. An old PRR station building, used by the mill for material storage, stood at the south ends of the main and finish yards, 4-6. Weirton Steel used the Conrail branch line as its main line but also had another main that reached a slag dump, which was run by Standard Slag Company. Situated just across the border in Pennsylvania, Standard Slag had two small GE diesels for switching.

The Weirton Steel railroad used radios for control with three yard-masters. By 1992, they consolidated

into one central dispatcher. There were 86 railroad crewmen who worked eight-hour shifts, or turns. The shifts included one 2-man crew for the blast furnaces, one 2-man crew for the slag train, three 3-man yard crews, and one 3-man crew at the ore yard. The blast furnace, slag, and ore yard crews usually got one Alco locomotive, while the yard crews typically got a pair of multiple-unit switchers or the S2 slug set.

Being an integrated steel mill, except for coke producing in the 1980s, the mill railroad had to haul a variety of

4-12

Norfolk Southern locomotives drag a freight train past the steel works at Mingo Junction, Ohio. *J. Alex Lang*

4-13

Steel slabs hang beneath the center line of this gigantic wheeled Kress slab carrier at Sparrows Point, Md. Wheeled vehicles are assuming a larger role in intra-plant steel movement.

4-14

The brick refractory lining is just visible above the pouring spout of this open-top ladle car. *Library of Congress*

4-15

Reichard Industries of Columbiana, Ohio, rebuilds hot metal cars and gives them snazzy paint jobs. Modeling a paint job like this would be appropriate for a new car being transferred to a mill, but the paint quickly wears away. *Chris Schmuck*

materials using specialized cars. Many of the intra-mill moves took various forms of steel—including slabs, ingots, coils, and sheet—to different finishing buildings. Then the finished loads went to the interchange yard or to the finished product warehouse.

Typical train size was 5 to 15 cars. Slag trains were usually 15 cinder pots long and created quite a display of sparks and flames at the dump area. The slag cools slightly as it sits in the cinder pot, so a gray crust forms on the top. But at the dump, the cars tipped over and orange, glowing, 2,000°F melted slag poured out from under the crust. After the open-hearth furnaces were shut down, Weirton sometimes used the empty building for dumping slag, **4-7**.

Since Walnut Street Yard was at the bottom of a short grade, the railroad had to use multiple unit sets of locomotives to bring inbound cars to the finish yard, **4-8**. Conrail delivered coal, coke, scrap, and limestone in hoppers,

covered hoppers, and gondolas to Walnut Street Yard.

Tapping the blast furnace was a dangerous job that required special procedures. The blast furnaces were located at the north end of the plant, while the basic oxygen furnace was to the south in the middle of the mill. The railroad transported the hot metal from the blast furnaces to the basic oxygen furnace in bottle cars. The 380-ton bottle cars were so heavy that they flattened the rails, which had to be replaced every five years.

When it was time to tap the furnace, the switcher positioned bottle cars under the appropriate runners in the cast house floor, **4-9**. A worker from the cast house clad in a silver protective suit stepped on the platform above the cars to ensure that the primary car and the extra car were in the proper positions. After the worker signaled, the locomotive uncoupled and pulled back a safe distance, **4-10**. Another locomotive similarly

positioned slag cars on the opposite side of the blast furnace under the slag runners, **4-11**. A klaxon sounded, and they tapped the furnace, which released a stream of glowing orange material that poured into the waiting bottle cars and cinder cars. It took nearly 10 minutes to complete the pour. The extra bottle car was used for any overflow.

Once the liquid metal and slag stopped flowing, the remotely controlled locomotive moved up and coupled to the bottle car or cinder car. They then slowly pulled the hot metal to the basic oxygen furnace at 10 mph, while the slag went to the dump. All other traffic on the adjacent tracks came to a halt out of respect for this cargo.

At the basic oxygen furnace, the locomotive backed the hot metal into the six-story-tall basic oxygen furnace. It retrieved any empty bottle cars and spotted the fresh hot metal. Once the basic oxygen furnace and continuous caster converted the iron to steel slabs, another locomotive hauled a train of hot steel slabs to the rolling mills for conversion to sheet tin.

In the 1980s, Conrail served Weirton with two regular trains, which picked up and set off at Walnut Street. One was WIMJ-30, a Mingo Junction-Weirton-Follansbee, W.Va., local, and WIMJ-32/WICE-33, a Mingo Junction-Weirton-Conway Yard, Pa., turnaround job. Conrail also delivered coke in special trains, as Weirton Steel bought this from outside sources after they closed their own coke works. Conrail also delivered iron ore from Mingo Junction by special moves that went directly into Weirton's ore yard, the only work Conrail did in the mill. Sometimes Conrail ran a local through the plant to Chester, W. Va., to switch the town there. This train passed through the steel mill.

Since Alco engine parts were hard to find, Weirton began replacing its old Alcos with newer locomotives. Weirton tested Electro-Motive GP38s but found them too big to work the entire plant as some curves were tight even for an S2. The first replacement came in 1985 when Weirton leased two Lake Erie, Franklin & Clarion SW1500s. Others were replaced at a rate of three or four per year with locomotives that included secondhand SW1500s from the Pittsburgh & Lake Erie.

With the closing of the hot end of the mill, the railroad became smaller. In 2009, the railroad had seven EMD SW1500s locomotives. They still use the main and junction yards to support the strip and tin mills. Norfolk Southern is now the interchange partner, **4-12**.

Steel mill freight cars

The need to haul big, heavy, and often very hot, hazardous loads led the steel industry to develop a variety of specialized railroad cars. They included hot metal cars called bottle, submarine, or torpedo ladle cars, cinder pots or slag cars, ladle cars, mill gondolas, covered coil gondolas, and mill flatcars. These railcars were the dominant form of intra-mill movement for more than 100 years. In the last few decades, rubber-tired vehicles have begun to replace some of the railcars, **4-13**.

4-16 NS 3040 with empty bottle cars from ArcelorMittal's East Chicago Plant 1 heads south through Plant 2 in March 2001. Note the spacer cars between the bottle cars. *Joel Hinkhouse*

4-17 Most steel mills have special heavy-duty flatcars to haul heavy slabs around the mill, such as this car at the coil yard at Sparrows Point, Md.

Hot metal cars

The first ironmakers let molten iron run out in puddles in front of the furnace to cool. The practice evolved into making a runner leading away from the furnace with short lateral runners off one side to mold the iron into a convenient shape for future handling. The whole arrangement roughly resembled a sow with a litter of suckling pigs, and from this practice came the term *pig iron*.

Once the pigs cooled, workers hauled them to cupola furnaces and melted the pigs before charging the steel converters. This was necessary because of the uneven composition of the molten iron. Each batch had to be analyzed, and batches blended together to make a mixture in the cupola suitable for use in the converters. However, it wasted an enormous amount of energy and labor to remelt the pigs and cast them.

The invention of the mixer by W. R. Jones in 1887 solved the problem by combining the small batches of iron in the mixer. The steel industry quickly developed specialized railroad cars to haul this molten metal. The first cars were relatively small, 10 tons or so, and resembled ladles on wheels.

There are three types of hot metal cars: the open-top ladle, the Kling-type ladle, and the mixer-type or Pugh car.

4-18

Ingot cars wait at Edgar Thompson steel works in Pennsylvania. *Library of Congress*

The open-top ladle car has a vessel that looks like an inverted bucket having trunnions on the sides with matching castings on the car frame to hold the vessel, **4-14**. The Kling-type ladle has a somewhat spherical shape with a smaller opening at the top. With the smaller opening, the hot metal loses less heat than it does in an open-top ladle car. Treadwell and Pollock were popular manufacturers of these early cars. State Tool & Die Company offers a Pollock Kling-type car and an open-top ladle car in HO scale. Trix makes open-top ladle cars in N and HO scales.

The Pugh car is now more commonly called a bottle, submarine, or torpedo ladle car. The first of these had a capacity of 150 tons, but current cars can haul up to 380 tons. These hot metal cars have a torpedo-shaped transfer vessel that is lined with refractory brick and supported on railroad trucks, sometimes with two or three at each end. During filling and transport, the opening on the barrel of the vessel, known as the pouring mouth, faces up. When the car is emptied, the vessel is rotated about its longitudinal axis by electric motors so the molten pig iron flows out of the opening into the mixer. Model railroad manufacturers offer models of several different types of these cars in most scales, **4-15**.

After the bottle cars get filled at a blast furnace with molten iron, locomotives haul them to a steel-making furnace. Because of the extreme weight and hazards of moving hot metal, railroads tend to use spacer or idler cars between the locomotive and the hot metal cars, **4-16**. Sometimes the car makes an intermediate stop on the way to the converter to treat the hot metal, typically to desulfurize the iron by inserting a lance into the vessel through the opening. This extra stop can be included in model railroad operations to add variety to the hot metal transport cycle.

In a typical steel works with multiple blast furnaces, several hot metal cars will circulate around the mill at the various stations. The total time for a hot metal move cycle averages about 15 hours, allowing 3 hours for filling, 6 hours for the outward journey, and 6 hours for return of the empty vessel. These average times may differ because they may make stops for various reasons during the cycle. Some mills transport hot metal long distances; for example, AK Steel, at times, sends hot metal from the works at Ashland, Ky., to Middletown, Ohio.

Some heat loss occurs during the outward journey but normally not enough to affect the hot metal. On an extremely long stop, the hot metal could cool down so it can no longer be processed in the steelmaking furnace and has to be poured back in the converter to reprocess. However, the steel industry has developed techniques to reheat hot metal in the ladle to avoid pour-backs. In rare cases, such as accidents or derailment, hot metal will eventually solidify, which ruins the bottle car, so the railroad makes every effort to avoid this.

Because of heat loss during the return journey, the refractory brick in the empty vessel cools down. This leads to a lower temperature of the pig iron when supplied to the steelmaking furnace, since the pig iron, when charged into the vessel at the blast furnace, loses heat to the brick. Also, if the brick cools too much during a long return journey, cracks may occur in the brick lining, thereby reducing the car's service life. Because of the hazards and heat sensitivity, hot metal cars must receive priority handling on a model railroad as they do on a prototype railroad.

Slag cars

In the early days of the blast furnace, slag was handled as clinker or ashes shoveled by hand. The workers tapped the slag out of the furnace with the iron, skimmed it off, and ran it a short distance into puddles to cool. Slag is very brittle when cold, so workers could easily break it up by hand and load it into wheelbarrows or carts with shovels and forks. The slag was dumped in convenient holes or low places near the furnace. When coke replaced charcoal as fuel, the quantity of slag produced per ton of iron increased, necessitating changes in the handling and disposing of slag.

One simple method for disposing of the slag involves letting it run into a special pit near the furnace to cool. After weathering for a few weeks, wrecking balls break it up so it can be loaded onto trucks or railcars for disposal or additional processing. Sometimes a mill will granulate the slag by spraying it with a stream of water as it pours onto the ground. This creates a mass of popcorn-like material that can be ground up and used in the manufacture of cement.

As early as 1880, steel works began transporting slag in a liquid state. The first liquid slag cars were rectangular tanks of steel plate lined with firebrick. The cars were mounted on railroad trucks, and they had a spout on each

4-19

Lightweight sheet-metal covers protect the steel coils inside these covered coil steel cars.

4-20

CSX developed a series of high-side, high-volume cars for coke hauling. Coke is lighter than coal, so these hoppers have extensions that provide more volume at the same weight.

side that closed by a hinged gate. These cars were not very satisfactory because the cooled slag stuck to the firebrick, which reduced the subsequent capacity of the car and made the gate mechanism unreliable.

To address these concerns, a side-tilting car with a cast-iron pot was developed and remains basically the same today. At first, they had the same shape as the steel-plate cars, with almost straight sides and a flat bottom, which provided maximum capacity. But as the sides became more tapered, the pots dumped cleaner and the skull fell out without

hand prodding. (Skull is the cooled residue of spilled hot metal or slag that builds up on objects.)

The pots evolved into cone-shaped vessels with a steep taper and a small rounded bottom. The firebrick lining was eliminated since the slag released from the bare iron more readily than from the brick. Steam was used to rotate the pot, so the dangerous task of turning the pots by hand was avoided, and modern cars operate pneumatically. Pollock and Treadwell both produced versions of these cars. Many model manufacturers offer slag car kits in HO, N, and O scales.

4-21

Hulett unloaders dip their articulated arm buckets into the hold of an ore carrier. *Library of Congress*

Mill gondolas and flatcars

Mill gondolas primarily serve the steel industry. They range from 48 to 65 feet long and have smooth interiors and various side heights. With heavy-duty, reinforced construction, they can accommodate 70 to 109 tons subject to 286,000 pounds gross weight on rail. Some are equipped with crossbars, load-restraining devices, or wooden troughs for special-purpose handling. They frequently have drop ends for hauling long pipes or steel members. When hauling long loads, flatcars are coupled to a mill gondola to allow room for the long overhang. Many mill railroads have their own mill gondolas for use on-site. These gondolas see heavy service and take on a very weathered and battered appearance.

Heavy-duty flatcars are in common use at steel mills for hauling heavy slabs and coils around the mill, **4-17**. In fact, among the first all-steel railroad cars made in the United States were 60-ton flatcars designed to haul wire rope for the Pennsylvania Railroad in 1887 and 40-ton flatcars used to carry armor plate for Carnegie Steel in 1894. Now, the typical mill slab flatcars are 30 to 40 feet long with reinforced center and side sills. On the deck of the car, the mill usually places steel bars to separate the hot slab from the deck. Some mills cover the deck with a layer of crushed

slag between the bars to insulate the deck from the hot slab. State Tool & Die makes an HO kit of a slab flatcar.

Another form of flatcar used during the ingot-casting era was an ingot car, **4-18**. These are shorter, heavy-duty cars with fittings to align the ingot molds. Typically the ingot cars stay in the mill, but some mills shipped ingots 100 miles or more in special insulated ingot gondolas. Ingot molds range in size from 2 tons to more than 150 tons for special large forgings. State Tool & Die offers ingot cars in HO scale, while Stewart Products offers an N scale car kit.

Coil cars

Since the 1960s, railroads have moved coil steel in specialized open or covered coil cars, **4-19**. They use covered coil cars when the steel's surface finish is very important and must be protected, such as cold-rolled steel for appliance, auto body, and tinplate stock. Open cars are used for steel when the surface finish isn't important because it's going to be rerolled, pickled and galvanized, or sandblasted later. Open cars allow coils to be loaded right off the production line while they are still quite hot. This speeds up delivery and can increase profits. If loaded into a closed car, the contained heat could damage the brake components or the

car structure itself. Several manufacturers offer open and closed coil cars in various scales.

Hoppers

The iron ore mines that supply most steel mills in the United States and Canada are located a considerable distance from the mill. Thus, the ore needs to be transported by rail, water, or a combination of both before reaching the mill. Weather conditions often prevent mining and transportation during the colder months, so it is necessary to store approximately half a year's supply adjacent to the furnaces. The railroads developed smaller, heavily built ore cars to ship raw iron ore. They do ship ore in standard hoppers, but the cars are not filled to the top as they reach the weight limit before the volume limit. To some trackside observers, these cars appear empty.

Coke and limestone, the other essential ingredients, are rarely stored in large quantities and are consumed as received. Common carrier railroads ship coal, coke, and limestone in standard rail hopper cars. Covered hoppers carry processed lime and other additives. Some railroads developed higher cubic capacity hopper cars to ship coke, as coke is less dense than coal, **4-20**.

Railroads will frequently seek out back haul arrangements, so their hoppers can be loaded with coal in one direction and ore in another to maximize car utilization.

Water transportation

Although this chapter focuses on steel mills and their railroads, I want to address the role maritime transport has in the steelmaking process. Many integrated steel mills have waterfront locations to take advantage of water transportation that includes barges, Great Lakes vessels, and oceangoing ships. Since many of the furnaces in this country receive ore from the Lake Superior District, I'll briefly describe ore transportation from there. Overseas shipments of ore are also possible.

Railroads take ore mined at the various iron ranges in Michigan and Minnesota, often in the form of taconite pellets, to harbors at the head

4-22

Railroad tracks extend underneath the Hulett unloader, allowing the cars to be loaded directly from the hoppers. *Library of Congress*

of Lake Superior. There, bottom-opening ore cars drop it into bins on long piers that generally extend into the harbor. Bulk-carrying boats capable of holding 20,000-70,000 net tons per trip take the ore from these piers to the various ports on the Great Lakes. These boats traditionally are 500-600 feet in length, but several newer ships are 1,000 feet long. Because these vessels must traverse the locks of the Great Lakes, they have bluff (broad) bows and are narrower and generally longer than similarly sized oceangoing freighters.

Ore has been unloaded in various ways. Early sail-powered ore boats relied on men to manually shovel the load into wheelbarrows. Gradually, steam power came into use with blocks and buckets rigged to ships' masts. In 1898, the Hulett unloader arrived and devoured its

(continued on page 54)

4-23

The *John L. Boland* self-unloading bulk carrier departs U.S. Steel at Zug Island after unloading a load of ore in June 2008. It was built by Bay Shipbuilding of Sturgeon Bay, Wis., and launched March 10, 1973, for the American Steamship Company of Buffalo, N.Y.

Ford's River Rouge plant

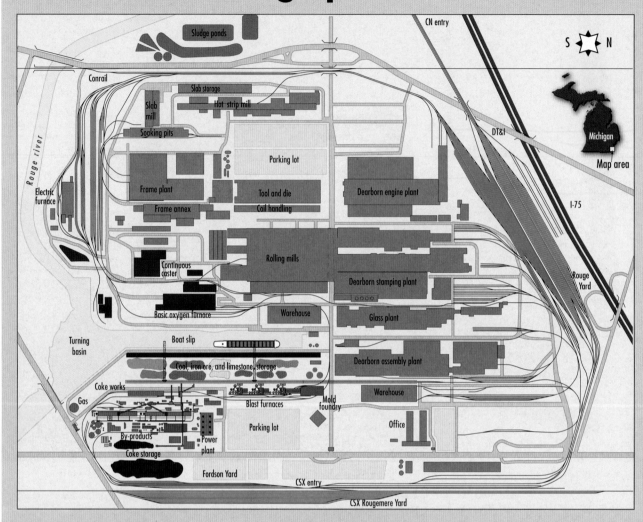

The Ford River Rouge complex may be the world's most famous auto plant. Famous architects designed some of the structures and famous photographers documented its scenes. Why all the fuss?

In 1915, Henry Ford bought 2,000 acres along the Rouge River west of Detroit, intending to use the site to produce coke, steel, and tractors. Over the next dozen years, however, the company turned The Rouge into the most fully integrated car manufacturing facility in the world. By 1927, the complex included virtually every element needed to produce a car: blast furnaces, an open-hearth mill, a steel rolling mill, stamping plants, a glass plant, a huge power plant and, of course, an assembly line. Ninety miles of

railroad track and miles more of conveyor belts connected these facilities.

Ford selected the site because of its central location, saying, "Up in northern Michigan and Minnesota are great iron ore deposits. Down in Kentucky and West Virginia are huge deposits of soft coal. Here we stand, half way between, with water transportation to our door. You will look the whole country over but you won't find a place that compares with this."

The first products out of The Rouge were not cars at all, but Eagle class ships for the U.S. Navy during WWI. But the emphasis switched to automobiles as soon as the war ended. The first of the Rouge's blast furnaces was finished in 1920, a second blast furnace was added

in 1922, and a third in 1948. They were named for Ford family members.

The first steel flowed out in 1923 from an electric furnace. Large capacity, open-hearth furnaces followed in 1926. In that year, The Rouge produced 321,476 tons of ingot steel, and output doubled within three years. By 1929, the manufacturing complex covered almost 1,200 acres of land, 350 of which were taken up by steelmaking facilities.

In 1964, two basic oxygen furnaces were installed, making use of 75 percent hot metal from the blast furnaces and 25 percent scrap. In 1976, two large electric arc furnaces, capable of producing 850,000 tons of steel per year, were added. Essentially a mini-mill alongside the existing mill, the

CSX SD50-2 works at Rougemere Yard in June 2008. Severstal Steel is rebuilding the blast furnace in the background.

Smoke curls from the hot metal car as a Rouge Steel switcher pulls it out of the blast furnace to the basic oxygen furnace.

A view across the boat slip of blast furnace row shows an ore bridge and piles of ore, coke, and limestone. *Library of Congress*

The cast house of the northern blast furnace has tracks running through it.

electric arc furnaces allowed Rouge a high level of flexibility to meet sudden increases in demand or cover maintenance periods of the blast furnaces.

The railroad was an important part of the complex. In 1920, Henry Ford purchased the Detroit, Toledo & Ironton Railroad in order to secure transportation to The Rouge and his other automobile manufacturing facilities. After investing heavily to improve it, he sold it to the Pennsylvania Railroad in 1928. However, The Rouge maintained its own railroad called the Ford Rouge Railroad or FRDX. The FRDX handled all in-plant switching moves as well as transfer runs to three neighboring railroad yards: Fordson Rougemere (now CSX) on the southeast, Conrail (formerly Michigan Central, now Norfolk Southern), and Rouge (now Canadian National) on the north.

The FRDX received its first diesel in 1931. By 1937, the railroad handled 1,100 cars daily with 12 diesel and 14 steam locomotives. The FRDX had complete servicing facilities that maintained the engines to a high state of cleanliness, with washings every other day.

Ford also owned a fleet of ore carriers and tugs to supply The Rouge with ore and other raw materials. The river had to be extensively dredged to provide access to the plant. In the process of dredging, the shortcut channel was cut and Zug Island was created.

Compact cars became popular during the fuel crunch of the late 1970s, and a surge in small imports from Japan intensified competition for car buyers. The combined effects of Rouge's increased steel capacity, import competition, and Ford's shift

to smaller vehicles put Rouge's operation in the red. In the 1980s, Ford sold off many of the specialty industries within the complex. The steel mill and railroad became Rouge Steel in 1984 and ended up in the hands of the Russian steel firm Severstal in 2004.

Ford remains the mill's largest customer, although it also sells to General Motors and Chrysler. The coke works was disassembled, along with some of the steelmaking buildings, but many of the complex's most important buildings still stand. The 1917 Dearborn assembly plant still houses the main assembly line. Today, Ford is reinvesting in the Rouge plant with an eye toward environmental consciousness and energy efficiency, but it is no longer the integrated marvel that it once was.

4-24

The *John Munson* demonstrates its self-unloader by dropping coal at a power plant on the Rouge River in 2008. It was built in 1952 as part of U.S. Steel's fleet.

(continued from page 51)
first boat of ore. These ungainly, self-propelled articulated cranes drop a bucket-equipped arm into a ship's hold and take out 20-ton bites of ore, **4-21**. The operator rides in a compartment near the bucket and controls its movement from this location. He moves the bucket downward through the open hatch of the vessel, takes a grab, and then deposits the load into a hopper, **4-22**. A rotating feeder under the hopper places the ore into a small car that runs to another hopper positioned over railroad cars or to an ore trench in the ore yard. The ore bridge then picks the ore from the ore trench and distributes it onto the ore pile. The Huletts remained in service until 1992, and only a few remain standing.

Some mills have an ore bridge that extends over the boat, allowing the ore-bridge bucket to unload the vessel. Also, if a mill is large enough, some use special unloading rigs. These unloading rigs perform the same function as the Huletts but differ somewhat in construction. Instead of the bucket being carried by a rigid arm, it hangs from a trolley resembling a crane trolley; consequently, it cannot be rotated and it cannot clean out the hold of the vessel as completely as could a Hulett. The crews then have to use a small bulldozer and hand labor to complete the job.

Most recent vessels are self-unloaders, so the crew can unload the vessel without any need for shore-side

4-25

Ken Larsen's HO scale steel mill features a waterfront scene with a nicely built Great Lakes boat. *Ken Larsen*

personnel or equipment, **4-23**. A ship's hold has tapered bottoms similar to the hoppers on a coal car. A system of conveyors mounted on top of the keel, along with an extendable conveyor mounted on a pivoting boom, moves the ore (or coal or grain). The ship can dock at any location that has a suitable land area to take its load, **4-24**. The boom swings over the shore and engages the conveyor systems. The loose ore flows via gravity to the bottom of the ship's hold, onto one conveyor system down the length of the ship, up another conveyor, and then onto the boom. The operator aims the boom and deposits the load in neat piles on the shore. The self-unloading system allows a 1,000-foot vessel to routinely discharge as much as 70,000 tons of iron ore or coal in less than

10 hours. Oceangoing bulk carrier ships tend to not have self-unloaders, but the piers they visit have conveyor systems that can reach into the ship and extract the cargo.

Including a model ore boat and unloading devices on a layout does not add a lot of operational interest, but they do add a huge amount of visual appeal, **4-25**. Furthermore, the challenge of building these models can add hours of enjoyment to building a steel mill layout. Whether these advantages are worth the significant space these models will claim on a layout is up to you. To make the decision easier, Walthers offers a model of a Hulett unloader in HO scale while Sylvan sells a Great Lakes boat suitable as an ore carrier in both N and HO scales. Bearco is another company that offers HO scale ore boats.

Track planning

5-1

This chapter looks at several different approaches of modeling a steel mill operation. It features lessons learned from existing layouts as well as designs that introduce new ideas. Plans include modular designs, modest layouts that fit a small bedroom, midsized plans, and several basement-filling dream layouts for the most dedicated steel mill modeler.

Modeling all aspects of an integrated steel mill in a compact area poses a challenge, and selective compression of the area, structures, and operations is usually required. Understanding how steel mills and railroads interact helps us know what features we need to incorporate in a plan, **5-1**. However, describing the actual car movements in and around a steel mill can be quite involved. You may choose to model the industries that require switching in a steel mill and car movements to whatever degree you see fit.

A Lehigh Valley RS-3 pulls loaded gondolas with steel pipe from a pipe mill building on Mike Pennie's N scale layout.

FIVE

The Sloss-Sheffield merchant iron works included two blast furnaces arranged around a complex system of stoves, burner sheds, and tanks. The extended cast houses enabled the mill to cast pig iron in long runners. *Library of Congress, HAER*

Modeling steel mill operations

In general, the mainline carrier spots incoming cars at the interchange yard. Local switchers, usually owned by the steel mill, sort the cars and bring them to the appropriate locations in the mill. Many large mills have smaller yards for each of the major operations. For example, some mills have a coil yard, where finished coil cars get loaded and stored, or a stockyard for scrap gondolas awaiting movement to the open hearth. Outgoing traffic includes gondolas carrying finished steel products and empty ore and coal hoppers.

Movements internal to the steel mill involve specialized cars shuttling back and forth over short distances. Hot metal cars or bottle cars bring molten pig iron from the blast furnace to the converter, while cinder pots or slag cars take slag to dump. After hot metal is converted to steel, either ingots move to the soaking pits or ladles go to a continuous caster. Some mills use flatcars to move slabs to their respective rolling mills. The steel converters receive scrap in gondolas and flux in covered hoppers.

In the model railroading sense, there are numerous internal customers that need to be served within a steel mill. For example, tank cars spotted at rolling mills provide lubrication and pickling oil for the machinery, and they can then haul off sludge and waste oil. Boxcars deliver refractory material (firebrick), packing and shipping supplies, repair parts, insulation, and all sorts of sundry items to keep the machines operational. At any given time, parts of a steel mill are always being rebuilt, which generates the need for cars loaded with construction materials. The switching of these jobs can be modeled using waybills and car forwarding just as any customer on a mainline model railroad.

From a model railroad perspective, the interchange traffic with the outside world can provide interesting operations. There is ample prototypical

justification for the high-traffic densities normally found on model railroads. Delivering the hundreds of tons of raw materials needed for each blast furnace will keep your mainline connections quite busy.

Let's look at some numbers. A blast furnace uses about 2.55 tons of raw materials for every ton of hot metal produced: 1.7 tons of ore, 0.55 tons of coke, and 0.30 tons of limestone flux. A typical furnace in the 1950s would produce about 2,000 to 3,000 tons of hot metal per day. The above table shows the tons of raw material required for the daily output. To calculate how many cars you would need for delivery, first decide the length of the day you want to simulate (let's assume a half day of 12 hours). If you are modeling a smaller furnace with 2,000 tons of hot metal a day, then you will be producing 1,000 tons of hot metal in a shift. This

Furnace output (tons daily)		Raw materials (tons daily)			
Hot metal	Slag	Ore	Coke	Limestone	Total
2,000	670	3,400	1,100	600	5,100
3,000	1,000	5,100	1,650	900	7,650

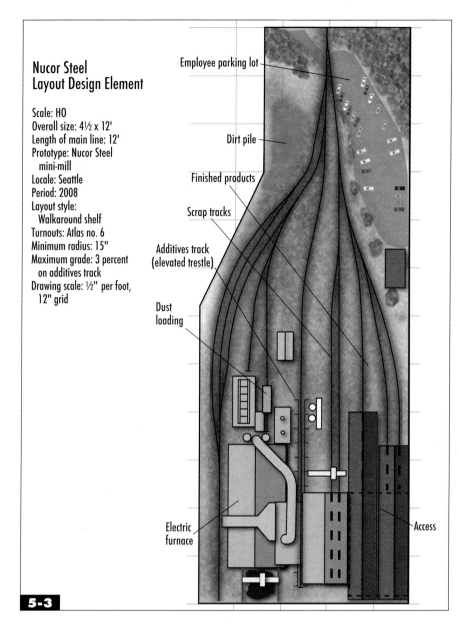

Nucor Steel
Layout Design Element

Scale: HO
Overall size: 4½ x 12'
Length of main line: 12'
Prototype: Nucor Steel
   mini-mill
Locale: Seattle
Period: 2008
Layout style:
   Walkaround shelf
Turnouts: Atlas no. 6
Minimum radius: 15"
Maximum grade: 3 percent
   on additives track
Drawing scale: ½" per foot,
   12" grid

Employee parking lot

Dirt pile

Finished products

Scrap tracks

Additives track
(elevated trestle)

Dust
loading

Electric
furnace

Access

5-3

5-4

A satellite view of the Nucor Steel mini-mill in Seattle, which lies across the bay from the downtown area. *USGS*

will require 1,700 tons of ore, 550 tons of coke, and 300 tons of limestone. If your cars have 100-ton capacity, that equates to 17 ore loads, 6 coke cars, and 3 limestone cars. On many integrated mills, coke is sent via conveyor from the coke works to the blast furnace, but for model railroads, it's more interesting to use hoppers to deliver the coke.

On the output side, operators typically tap a furnace every 3.5 hours. To keep the math simple, let's assume a 4-hour tap cycle. That works out to six taps a day, or three in the shift we are modeling. With each tap producing about 330 tons of hot metal, two 200-ton bottle cars must be spotted at the furnace three times during the shift.

Similarly, slag must be hauled off. In a half-day shift, our furnace will create 335 tons of slag with a volume of about 4,500 cubic feet. If using slag cars to haul the slag to the dump, you will need about 12 slag cars per shift or two per tap since a slag car can carry about 400 cubic feet. In any case, the furnace should not be left without at least two slag cars at any time, as slag can be tapped more frequently if using the cinder notch method. Instead of using slag cars, a modeled furnace may use a slag pit serviced by railcars, so you will need to spot four 100-ton hoppers per shift at the slag pit to haul out the cooled and broken-up slag. A slag pit usually has the capacity to hold slag from several taps, so it doesn't need to be serviced as regularly as when using hot slag cars.

Other incoming traffic includes coal for coke ovens and local power generation, scrap, and other mill supplies. The coke ovens yield about 0.7 tons of coke per ton of coal. On average, a model coke works will consume about 785 tons of coal per 12-hour shift to support the 1,000 tons of hot metal the blast furnace will produce. The by-product plant's main output by volume is gas, most of which gets burned in the mill. However, about 25 tons of tar and 5 tons of ammonium sulfate and other chemicals must be hauled out in the 12-hour shift.

The steel convertors need scrap to mix with hot metal when making steel. About one-quarter to one-third of a charge to an open hearth or basic oxygen furnace is scrap. So the 1,000 tons of hot metal delivered to the convertor will need about 250-330 tons of scrap, which can be rounded off to 300 tons as some of the scrap gets converted to slag and gas. Thus, our mill will produce about 1,300 tons of steel per 12-hour shift. The

5-5

The electric arc furnace building at Nucor Steel features exposed ducts and piping. The scrap crane in the foreground is an interesting detail to model.

5-6

A small Nucor switcher works the storage yard just north of the Nucor Steel mini-mill in Seattle. Note the buildings in the background.

convertors also consume about 100 tons of flux per shift.

Empty gondolas, flatcars, and coil cars must be provided so that finished steel can be shipped out. Mills frequently stockpile finished steel, so the layout operator can be flexible in scheduling outbound shipments, as long as provisions for shipping the daily output is maintained over the long haul. Using 1,300 tons per shift as our example, at 100 tons per car, you will need 13 cars, assuming it is all rail-shipped.

In summary, for a 12-hour shift, assuming all cars have a 100-ton capacity, our modest steel mill will require 17 loaded ore cars, 8 loaded coal hoppers, 4 limestone hoppers and 3 scrap gondolas. It will ship out 13 loaded coil cars or flatcars with finished steel, one tank car of tar, a boxcar of bagged chemicals, and 5 hoppers of slag.

Having an equal number of empties means about 100 cars move to and from the mill in a single shift per blast furnace. Scale this up for multiple blast furnaces and/or higher production rates, and the need to selectively compress becomes obvious. Throw in the intra-mill movements of coke, hot metal, slag, ingots, slabs, and scrap, and you have the makings of a busy operating session.

Merchant mill

For a module or small space on a layout, a merchant blast furnace may be appropriate. A merchant blast furnace is a stand-alone facility that produces pig iron for shipment and further processing at other remotely located plants. You could cram such a structure on a 2 x 4 module, but a larger module would allow room for a more believable length, sidings, and other components.

The Sloss-Sheffield Steel & Iron works in Birmingham, Ala., is an example of a fairly large merchant pig iron operation, 5-2. The twin blast furnaces made pig iron to support the numerous foundries in the local area. The main structure, although compact, is still fairly large. The twin furnace design is roughly symmetrical, so to save space, you could model only half the works and use a mirror or backdrop photos to simulate the rest. The Sloss-Sheffield works is now a preserved historical landmark and is worth a visit to anyone interested in steel mills.

Electric furnace mini-mill

Another way to model steel in a compact space is by adding a contemporary mini-mill that features an electric arc furnace and adjacent mills. Although it lacks the signature blast furnace, a mini-mill presents an interesting visual element as well as operational opportunity.

Figure 5-3 shows an example of a layout design element (LDE) based on the Nucor Steel mini-mill in Seattle, Wash., 5-4. This compact rail-served facility specializes in making bars and angles from scrap steel for customers in the Pacific Northwest. The electric arc furnace lies adjacent to the tracks. This mill has an exposed intricate down-comer and some complex scrap-handling cranes that are interesting to model, 5-5.

A compact yard to the northwest supports the mill, 5-6. This yard is adjacent to a large Class I railroad intermodal terminal, absolute heaven for the modern, heavy industry modeler. On the east side is an array of switch leads and tracks that serve the various spots on the mill. The plan shows a linear LDE for a 4 x 12-foot space. Because the mini-mill has the buildings clustered in a single group, the plan is fairly wide so it can include the furnace and rolling mill buildings. While this makes an impressive and prototypically realistic scene, it makes access to the back difficult if the layout design element is against a wall. In that case, access to the lower right corner is provided by a lift-out panel hidden by the rolling mill structures.

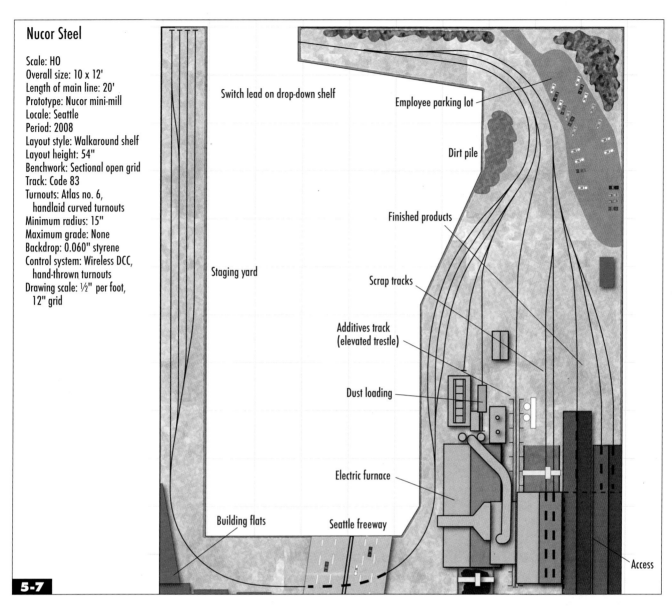

Nucor Steel

Scale: HO
Overall size: 10 x 12'
Length of main line: 20'
Prototype: Nucor mini-mill
Locale: Seattle
Period: 2008
Layout style: Walkaround shelf
Layout height: 54"
Benchwork: Sectional open grid
Track: Code 83
Turnouts: Atlas no. 6,
   handlaid curved turnouts
Minimum radius: 15"
Maximum grade: None
Backdrop: 0.060" styrene
Control system: Wireless DCC,
   hand-thrown turnouts
Drawing scale: ½" per foot,
   12" grid

Switch lead on drop-down shelf

Employee parking lot

Dirt pile

Finished products

Scrap tracks

Additives track
(elevated trestle)

Dust loading

Electric furnace

Staging yard

Building flats

Seattle freeway

Access

5-7

5-8

Monroe Stewart's layout includes a long, narrow steel mill scene behind the staging yard on the west end.

5-9

The Alkem Steel module used HO steel mill structures converted to N scale.

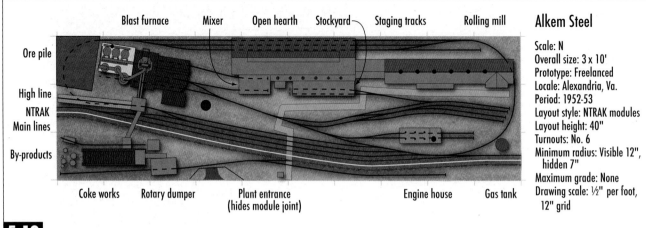

Ore pile

High line
NTRAK
Main lines

By-products

Blast furnace — Mixer — Open hearth — Stockyard — Staging tracks — Rolling mill

Coke works — Rotary dumper — Plant entrance (hides module joint) — Engine house — Gas tank

Alkem Steel

Scale: N
Overall size: 3 x 10'
Prototype: Freelanced
Locale: Alexandria, Va.
Period: 1952-53
Layout style: NTRAK modules
Layout height: 40"
Turnouts: No. 6
Minimum radius: Visible 12", hidden 7"
Maximum grade: None
Drawing scale: ½" per foot, 12" grid

5-10

5-11

The scratchbuilt coke works of Alkem Steel feeds coal to the blast furnace using a conveyor.

It is possible with some minor rearranging of the yard leads to incorporate the Nucor mini-mill LDE into a 10 x 12-foot bedroom layout, **5-7**. The curve leading to the staging yard runs under the Seattle freeway. The backdrop behind the staging yard should be painted with a low, forested ridge and lined with building flats to represent the hillside, warehouses, and homes that occupy the actual location. If desired, a track could connect the staging yard to the switching lead of the mill and provide a continuous run option.

Steel mill interchange yard
Another modeling approach is to build a mill interchange yard in the foreground and place the mill in the background. So instead of a distant ridge or building flats, mill structures

provide a dramatic backdrop. Monroe Stewart used this approach in his steel mill design, **5-8**. His scratchbuilt mill structures present an imposing industrial skyline behind the staging tracks of his layout.

You could take this concept a bit further by using the steel mill as an interchange destination. On this layout, you do not model all the switching that goes on in a steel mill. You would primarily model the mainline railroad bringing in loads of raw materials and empties for finished products. The mainline trains would take off empty hoppers and loaded steel products. You could also model the classification process in the yard and perhaps have the yard engines drag cars off to a hidden staging yard that would simulate the steel mill. The mill and

interchange yards can also be immediately adjacent as Rouge Steel's Fordson Yard is to the CSX Rougemere Yard.

The interchange does not have to be near the steel mill, but it would be more interesting if the steel mill were at least represented on the backdrop, either hand-painted or through photos. Several manufacturers offer backdrops with steel mill scenes for this purpose. Monroe pasted photos of his own mill structures to the wall as his backdrop images.

Complete steel mill operation
Several different types of plans address building a layout that features an integrated steel mill operation.

A modular steel mill. When Walthers first introduced the HO steel mill series of kits in 1996, I built a steel mill module around them, **5-9**. I built the steel mill on a NTRAK module, so it would be portable in case I moved or displayed it in public. While I could have built a portable, stand-alone layout, I concluded that a NTRAK module would be the best way to remain portable and perhaps improve operational possibilities by tying the module into a larger transportation system and having other NTRAK modules provide staging, **5-10**.

I made a 3 x 10-foot module base of two 3 x 5 sections with folding legs. One 3 x 5 module fit in my car, so I reasoned that, if necessary, I could take the modules to local shows by making two trips or by renting a trailer for longer distances.

The module depicted an integrated steel mill in which the manufacturing process flows from left to right. Coke is produced in the left front. The blast furnace on the left melts the ore. The pig iron flows to the right into the open hearth and from there to the rolling mills. I did not model the ingot-shifting and slab-moving operations, letting them take place off the layout. Finished coils are loaded on the rear right-hand tracks. Although the overall module is freelanced, several proto-typical structures provided the basis for my structures including an AK steel blast furnace, the open hearth at Weirton Steel, and elements of the Sparrows Point rolling mills.

The open hearth, with its distinctive row of parallel stacks, was a common sight in a 1950s steel mill. I included one of these plus a rolling mill. Together, they provided a long, massive structure that served as a scenic divider. The Walthers HO rolling mill kit makes a good starting point for many N scale mill structures. I used five of these as the basis for the rolling mill and the open hearth. (This process is described in more detail in Chapter 7.) The Walthers electric furnace is an even larger kit structure and might be suitable for modeling an N scale basic oxygen furnace, but since I was model-ing the 1950s, I did not use that kit.

While the module was NTRAK compatible, it could be operated in a realistic manner as a stand-alone layout. The track plan included arrival and departure tracks for incoming and outgoing trains, a small stub-ended classification yard to sort cars, a three-track staging yard partially hidden in the open hearth, and several sidings where cars are spotted. The table lists some of the car types that were spotted at each siding.

The module set had a continuous loop for display at shows, and an automated high line used a Circuitron auto reverse circuit to provide an additional action element. In the foreground, I scratchbuilt a coke works, using Dean Freytag's plans, **5-11**, and an operational rotary dumper.

There was no skyboard. The struc-tures acted as the view block. All of the prototypes I emulated were on fill land, so the module had little vertical relief in

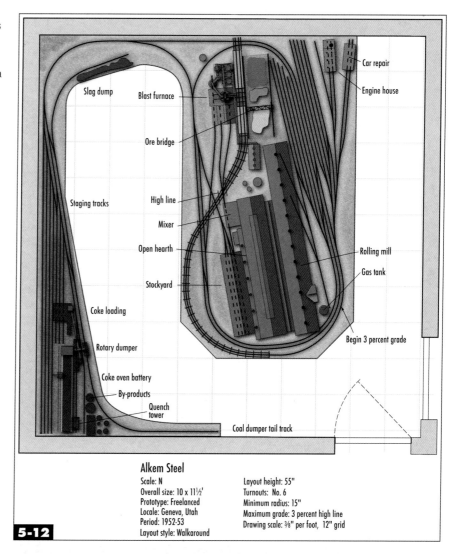

Alkem Steel

Scale: N
Overall size: 10 x 11½'
Prototype: Freelanced
Locale: Geneva, Utah
Period: 1952-53
Layout style: Walkaround

Layout height: 55"
Turnouts: No. 6
Minimum radius: 15"
Maximum grade: 3 percent high line
Drawing scale: ⅜" per foot, 12" grid

5-12

Location	Type of cars spotted
Ash track	Covered hoppers
Slag track	Slag cars
Ore/stone tipple	Ore and stone hoppers
Coil yard	Coil cars and flatcars
Stock house	Scrap gondolas
Sludge track	Oil tank cars
Stripping tracks (rear staging tracks)	Ingot cars
Engine service tracks	Locomotive and service and repair cars

terrain. A drainage canal exited the front and provided a nice foreground location for details.

Since I built this module before Walthers released the N scale version of their steel mill series, I used HO structures. A chief concern I had was reducing the visual scale of the HO kit structures, but several design features helped provide the right sense of scale. The foreground included highly

detailed N scale structures, such as the coke works and the engine house, as well as lots of N scale clutter. The coarser HO scale structures, embel-lished with N scale details, lined the background. In a few places, N scale structures abutted the HO kits to help provide additional visual cues to scale down the structures. The HO structures incorporated numerous roof lines,

(continued on page 65)

Calumet Steel

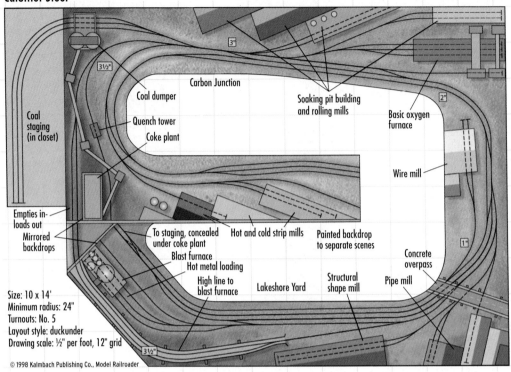

Carbon Junction

Coal dumper

Quench tower

Coke plant

Coal staging (in closet)

Soaking pit building and rolling mills

Basic oxygen furnace

Wire mill

Empties in-loads out

Mirrored backdrops

To staging, concealed under coke plant

Blast furnace

Hot metal loading

High line to blast furnace

Hot and cold strip mills

Lakeshore Yard

Painted backdrop to separate scenes

Structural shape mill

Pipe mill

Concrete overpass

Size: 10 x 14'
Minimum radius: 24"
Turnouts: No. 5
Layout style: duckunder
Drawing scale: ½" per foot, 12" grid

Pittsburgh Steel

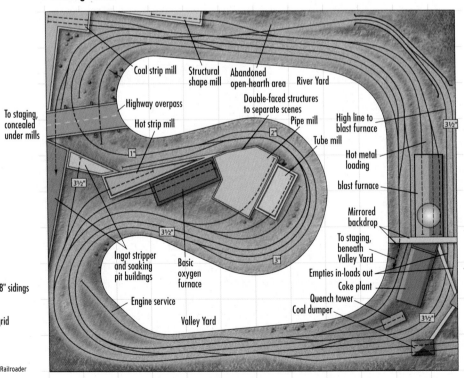

Coal strip mill

Structural shape mill

Abandoned open-hearth area

River Yard

Highway overpass

Double-faced structures to separate scenes

Pipe mill

High line to blast furnace

To staging, concealed under mills

Hot strip mill

Tube mill

Hot metal loading

blast furnace

Mirrored backdrop

Ingot stripper and soaking pit buildings

Basic oxygen furnace

To staging, beneath Valley Yard

Empties in-loads out

Coke plant

Engine service

Quench tower

Coal dumper

Valley Yard

Size: 10 x 12'
Minimum radius: 20" mainline, 18" sidings
Turnouts: No. 4 and 5
Layout style: Duckunder
Drawing scale: ½" per foot, 12" grid

5-13

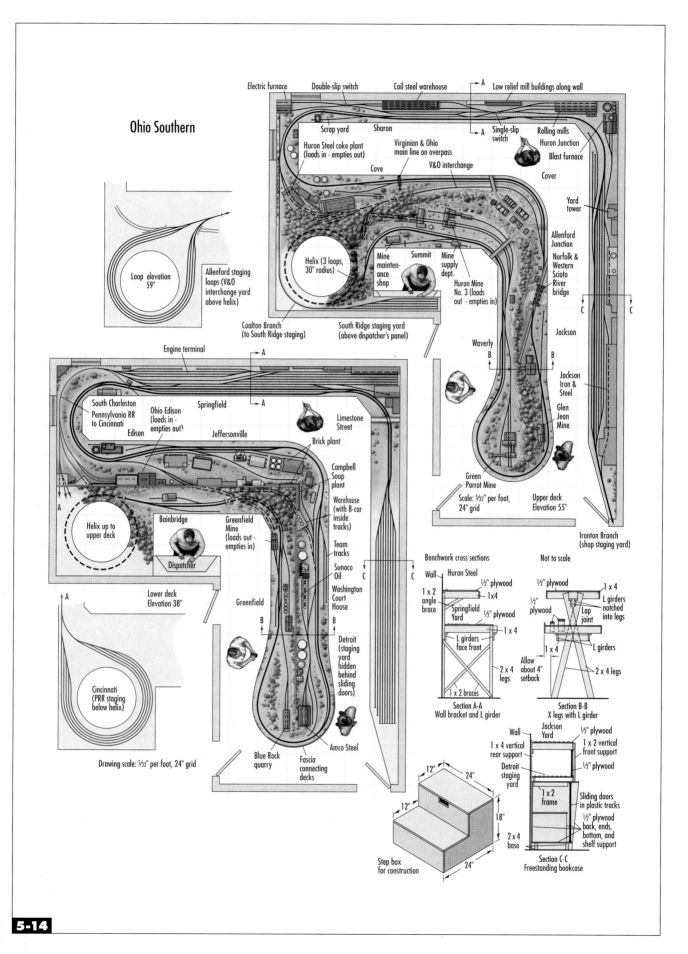

Ohio Southern

Electric furnace
Double-slip switch
Coil steel warehouse
A
Low relief mill buildings along wall
Scrap yard
Sharon
A
Single-slip switch
Rolling mills
Huron Junction
Huron Steel coke plant (loads in - empties out)
Virginian & Ohio main line on overpass
Blast furnace
Cove
V&O interchange
Cover
Yard tower
Helix (3 loops, 30" radius)
Mine maintenance shop
Summit
Mine supply dept.
Allenford Junction
Huron Mine No. 3 (loads out - empties in)
Norfolk & Western Scioto River bridge
C
C
Jackson
Coalton Branch (to South Ridge staging)
South Ridge staging yard (above dispatcher's panel)
Waverly
B
B
Jackson Iron & Steel
Glen Jean Mine
Green Parrot Mine
Scale: ⁵⁄₃₂" per foot, 24" grid
Upper deck Elevation 55"
Ironton Branch (shop staging yard)

Loop elevation 59"
Allenford staging loops (V&O interchange yard above helix)

Engine terminal
A
A
South Charleston Pennsylvania RR to Cincinnati
Ohio Edison (loads in - empties out)
Springfield
Edison
Jeffersonville
Limestone Street
Brick plant
Campbell Soup plant
Warehouse (with 8-car inside tracks)
Team tracks
Sunoco Oil
Washington Court House
C
C
Helix up to upper deck
Bainbridge
Greenfield Mine (loads out - empties in)
Dispatcher
Greenfield
B
B
Detroit (staging yard hidden behind sliding doors)
Lower deck Elevation 38"
A
Blue Rock quarry
Fascia connecting decks
Amco Steel
Cincinnati (PRR staging below helix)
Drawing scale: ⁵⁄₃₂" per foot, 24" grid

Benchwork cross sections
Not to scale

Wall
Huron Steel
½" plywood
1 x 2 angle brace
1x4
Springfield Yard
½" plywood
L girders face front
1 x 4
2 x 4 legs
1 x 2 braces
Section A-A
Wall bracket and L girder

½" plywood
1 x 4
½" plywood
Lap joint
L girders notched into legs
Allow about 4" setback
1 x 4
L girders
2 x 4 legs
Section B-B
X legs with L girder

Wall
Jackson Yard
½" plywood
1 x 4 vertical rear support
1 x 2 vertical front support
Detroit staging yard
½" plywood
1 x 2 frame
Sliding doors in plastic tracks
½" plywood back, ends, bottom, and shelf support
2 x 4 base
Section C-C
Freestanding bookcase

12"
24"
12"
18"
24"
Step box for construction

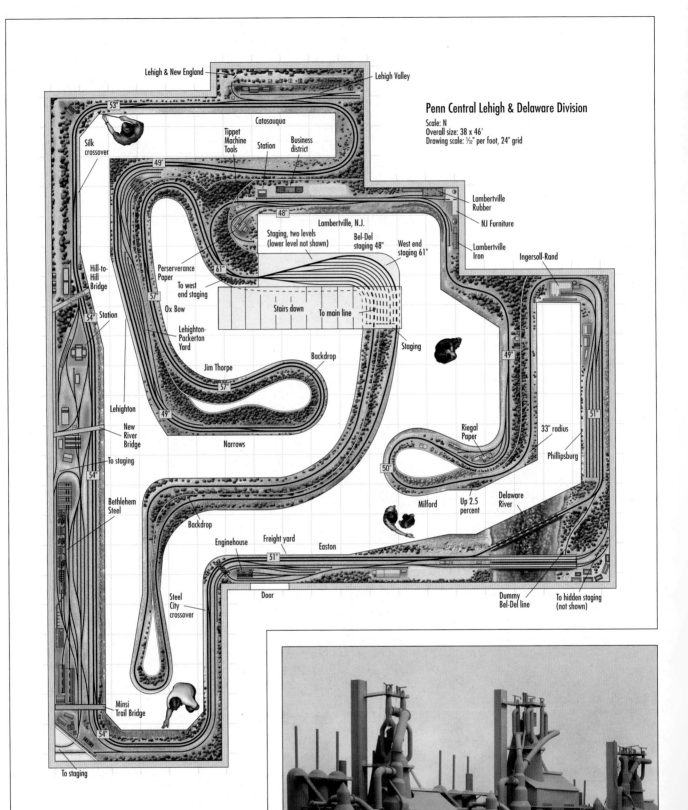

Lehigh & New England

Lehigh Valley

53"

Silk crossover

Catasauqua

Tippet Machine Tools

Station

Business district

Penn Central Lehigh & Delaware Division

Scale: N
Overall size: 38 x 46'
Drawing scale: 5/32" per foot, 24" grid

49"

Lambertville Rubber

NJ Furniture

48"

Lambertville, N.J.

Hill-to-Hill Bridge

Perserverance Paper

61"

Staging, two levels (lower level not shown)

Bel-Del staging 48"

West end staging 61"

Lambertville Iron

Ingersoll-Rand

54" Station

57"

Ox Bow

To west end staging

Stairs down

To main line

Staging

49"

Lehighton-Packerton Yard

Jim Thorpe

Backdrop

51"

Lehighton

57"

New River Bridge

49"

Narrows

Riegal Paper

33" radius

Phillipsburg

To staging

54"

50"

Up 2.5 percent

Delaware River

Bethlehem Steel

Backdrop

Milford

Enginehouse

Freight yard

Easton

Steel City crossover

51"

Minsi Trail Bridge

Door

Dummy Bel-Del line

To hidden staging (not shown)

54"

To staging

5-16

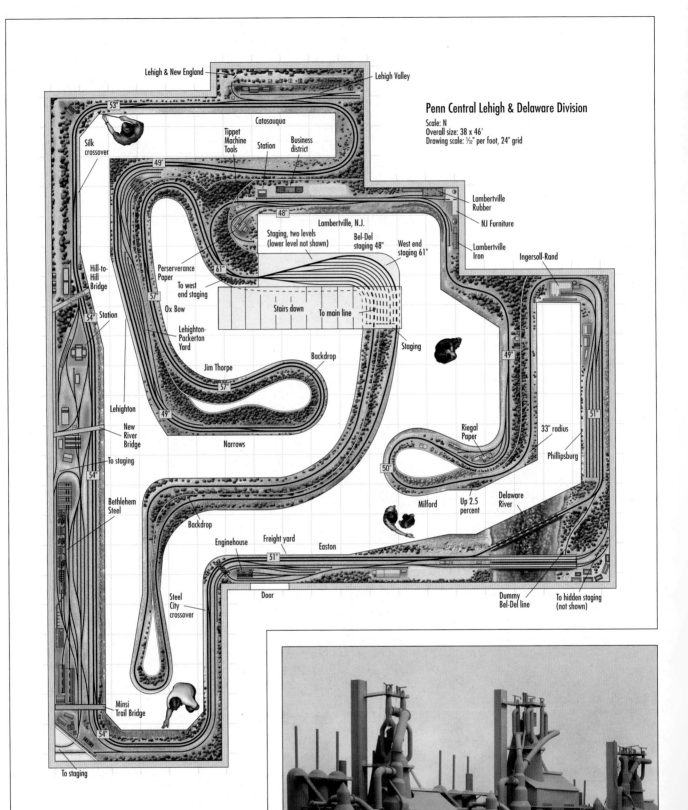

5-17

Mike Pennie built most of these mill structures from scratch.

5-15

Due to the narrow shelf, Jim Hediger relies on low-relief buildings to represent the rolling mill structures. In spite of their shallow depth, they present an imposing presence. *Jim Hediger*

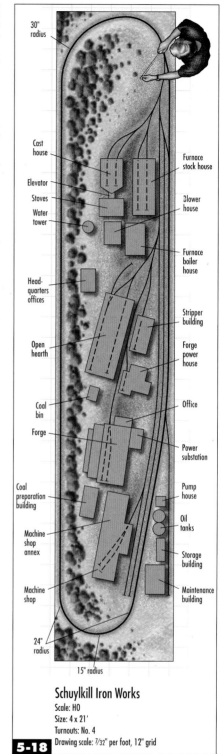

Schuylkill Iron Works
Scale: HO
Size: 4 x 21'
Turnouts: No. 4
Drawing scale: 7/32" per foot, 12" grid

5-18

(continued from page 61)
gables, craneways, and vents to break up the mass and provide visual interest. Heavy weathering and common paint schemes helped blend everything together. The desired effect was to keep focus on the N scale detail in the foreground. Then the eye automatically assumes and extrapolates that level of detail to the background structures.

Bedroom-sized steel mill layouts.
In 1999, I designed an N scale steel mill layout for *Model Railroad Planning* that utilized a 5 x 9-foot table as a base, **5-12**. That plan utilized a hidden staging area under a removable town section. While this design worked, given the tight design constraint of a 5 x 9 table, a better plan would be to use the 5 x 9 table as a peninsula in a 10 x 12-foot room and use the perimeter of the room for layout expansion.

I moved the staging area from the hidden location under the town to a narrow shelf on the wall, which improved the layout immeasurably. This allowed better access for the staging tracks, provided less crowding around the elevated high line, and offered switching opportunities for additional industries. The revised plan shows a coke works and slag dump. I also

redesigned the track plan to take advantage of the extra space and to use the N scale kits that are now available.

I loosely based this plan after the Geneva Steel mill just south of Salt Lake City, which has since been torn down. This track plan reminded me of the pinched oval-triangular configuration of the Geneva mill trackwork with the D&RGW on the west, the UP on the right, and a connecting loop track to the north. However, the actual mill had a line of three blast furnaces, not just the one I show. You could imply the extra furnaces by using a mirror or backdrop painting. To simulate the service from two separate railroads, a second staging yard could be added to the right wall to provide staging for the separate railroads.

Bedroom-sized steel mill layout plans are not restricted to N scale. *Model Railroader* magazine has featured two notable plans by Darius Chagnon for room-sized layouts in HO scale. The first fits in a 10 x 12-foot area while the second requires a 10 x 14-foot room, **5-13**. Both plans feature representations of integrated steel mills using basic oxygen furnaces for steel conversion. The plans employ hidden staging under the layout for off-layout destinations, but

they use loads in/empties out to simplify the staging of the blast furnace high line tracks and coke plant. Since the ore and limestone usually arrive in open-top loads, some method of removing the load during a session is required if you wish to model multiple casts at the blast furnace. Otherwise, cars at these spots can only make one-half of a cycle during

5-19

Eric Craig's Schuylkill Iron Works features numerous scratchbuilt stone and brick structures for his early 20th century steel mill layout. *Eric Craig*

an operating session. In other words, a session entails just pulling empties at the blast furnace and replacing them with loads. For a smaller layout, this is probably acceptable.

The smaller of the two plans features an area for a former open-hearth structure. However, including an abandoned open-hearth structure would not be unreasonable since they tended to remain standing long after they went out of service. Modeling it in a state of partial disassembly might be an interesting modeling challenge.

Narrow shelf designs. Narrow shelf layouts are becoming increasing popular as they maximize the length of a mainline run for a given space. Furthermore, they are almost mandatory in multiple deck designs.

Jim Hediger's freelanced, double-deck Ohio Southern HO layout devotes a considerable portion of the upper deck to steel mill operation, **5-14**. His plan includes coke works, rolling mills, warehouses, a blast furnace, and an electric furnace. He does not include an open hearth or basic oxygen furnace, so his switching operations focus on

raw materials in and finished steel products out. The intra-mill switching moves hot metal from the blast furnace to the electric furnace and then to the slab caster. Additional movements are assumed to take place behind the backdrop into Jackson Iron & Steel's rolling mills. This is an excellent trick to use in keeping the steel mill operation manageable on a layout that also features a considerable mainline run.

Because he has a narrow shelf to work with, Jim's structures tend to be low-relief buildings set against the backdrop wall. These low-relief buildings are not quite flat, having about two or three inches of depth, **5-15**. For the slab-sided rolling mill structures found at a steel mill, this is sufficient to convey the full scope of the structure, especially when installed on an upper deck at near eye-level height. He situated his blast furnace and electric arc furnaces in corners where he had more room to fit the Walthers kit-based models.

Mike Pennie's N scale layout uses a similar approach, but since the layout is a smaller scale, he can fit more of the actual structures on his shelf, **5-16**. He

models the Bethlehem Steel mill along the former Penn Central in a slightly freelanced arrangement. Mike scratch-built all his blast furnace models, as he built them before the Walthers kits were released, **5-17**.

Midsized and larger designs. Eric Craig's HO plan for his Schuylkill Iron Works occupies a 4 x 21-foot space along a single wall, **5-18**. The plan includes an oval for continuous running. It would be a simple matter to expand the layout in either direction by adding turnouts at the loop ends. The plan includes a complete integrated steel mill having one blast furnace, an open hearth with four furnaces, a forge, and numerous supporting buildings. Eric elected to model the early 20th century, **5-19**. By doing so, he took advantage of the smaller size of the structures that were used at the time, and he was able to fit a complete mill in 84 square feet. The disadvantage is that he had to either scratchbuild or kitbash all of the stone and brick structures.

The plan of Ford's Rouge Steel shows a midsized layout design for a 12 x 21-foot garage-sized space, **5-20**. The plan has a central peninsula depicting the blast furnaces, coke works, and power plant. The drawing includes the ore pile and a boat slip. As a result, the left aisle is a bit tight. For more room, the boat slip and/or ore pile could be dropped from the plan, which would reduce the overall layout width by 2 feet and leave enough space for a 3-foot aisle. You could also make the boat slip and ore pile removable for operating sessions as Ken Larsen does on his lakefront steel mill layout (see page 54). However, part of the charm of a steel mill layout is the challenge of building the intricate models, and the model-building opportunity for the boat and ore pile with ore bridges is too good to pass up.

Even with selective compression and omitting a blast furnace, the kit blast furnaces will need a degree of custom building for the cast houses to work in this plan. The cast houses on the Walthers models do not really fit here. The Rogue Steel map (page 52) gives you a better idea of how the hot metal and slag tracks pass under the cast house. The model plan tries to capture this in the limited space. The northernmost cast house incorporates the track cutting through the corner of the building as in the prototype.

The layout plan combines several yards surrounding the mill into a single four-track yard at Rougemere with a track for high line access. The current mill, now called Severstal North America, has a conveyor system for furnace charging instead of the high line. The coke works has also been torn down. This layout plan predates those modifications.

There is a fairly small part of the layout devoted to the Ford automobile assembly and shipping aspect of The Rouge. You could easily take the opposite tack and focus on this part of the operation, but this plan emphasizes the steel side of the business. In any case, the assembly plants would receive hi-cube boxcars of auto parts, while finished vehicles, either Mustangs or pick-up trucks depending on the era, can be loaded at the autorack tracks.

Jeff Bourne's freelanced Twin Cities & Western Railroad serves several heavy industries including Columbia River Steel, a notional company with steel mills in Minnesota and Washington. Nearly half of the basement-filling layout is devoted to the Columbia steel and nickel divisions, **5-21**. His structures are all scratchbuilt and incredibly detailed, **5-22**. While his layout focuses on heavy industries, he also includes partial main lines for two railroads, the Milwaukee Road and the Twin Cities & Western. The Milwaukee Road

Rouge Steel

Scale: HO
Overall size: 12 x 21'
Prototype: Rouge steel
Locale: Dearborn, Mich.
Period: 1999
Layout style: Walkaround

Layout height: 55"
Turnouts: No. 6
Minimum radius: 18 inches
Maximum grade: 3.5 percent highline
Drawing scale: 5/16" per foot, 12" grid

Warehouse
Rolling mills
Blast furnaces
High line trestle
Ore bridges
Fordson Yard
Power plant
Basic oxygen furnace
Rougemere Yard
Begin high line grade
Ore boat
Coke works
Electric furnace
By-products
Autorack loading
Assembly plants

5-20

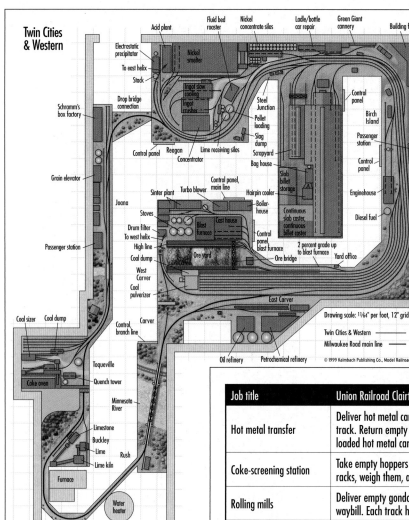

Twin Cities & Western

Acid plant · Fluid bed roaster · Nickel concentrate silos · Ladle/bottle car repair · Green Giant cannery · Building flats

Electrostatic precipitator · Nickel smelter · To east helix · Stack · Drop bridge connection · Ingot slow cooling · Ingot crusher · Steel Junction · Birch Island · Control panel · Pellet loading · Passenger station · Control panel · Schramm's box factory · Control panel · Reagan Concentrator · Lime receiving silos · Slag dump · Scrapyard · Bag house · Slab billet storage · Grain elevator · Sinter plant · Turbo blower · Control panel, main line · Hairpin cooler · Boiler house · Continuous slab caster, continuous billet caster · Enginehouse · Joana · Stoves · Drum filter · To west helix · Blast furnace · Cast house · Control panel, blast furnace · 2 percent grade up to blast furnace · Diesel fuel · Passenger station · High line · Coal dump · Ore yard · Ore bridge · Yard office · West Carver · Coal pulverizer · Carver · East Carver · Coal sizer · Coal dump · Control, branch line · Toqueville · Quench tower · Minnesota River · Limestone · Buckley · Lime · Rush · Coke oven · Lime kiln · Furnace · Water heater

Drawing scale: 11/64" per foot, 12" grid
Twin Cities & Western ——
Milwaukee Road main line ——

Oil refinery · Petrochemical refinery · © 1999 Kalmbach Publishing Co., Model Railroader

5-21

portion exists on the layout as a smaller loop, primarily to interchange with the Twin Cities & Western. The latter railroad has a longer mainline run that crosses the Minnesota River to reach a coke works and a typical Midwestern town. He plans to add two additional blast furnaces using modified versions of the Walthers HO kit.

Tom Wilson built a double-deck HO scale model railroad that fills a two-car garage, **5-23**. The upper level of the layout is devoted primarily to the Union Railroad and U.S. Steel Clairton Coke Works. Tom worked for several years at the Clairton Coke Works, and he based his layout on the prototype, although with significant selective compression. To depict the Clairton works, he utilizes a single yard for his steel mill traffic as opposed to the numerous yards that exist on the

prototype. Likewise, he had to compress the industries. The actual coke works at Clairton, if modeled one-to-one, would have taken up nearly two times the area Tom had available. So he chose to use the coke works at Thomas, Ala., as a guide for his coke works model, although he did include the quenching towers and coke wharfs from the Clairton Coke Works.

Tom's railroad is fully operational, and he hosts operating sessions regularly. One of the dangers of steel mill modeling is that operations can get stale if each crew is assigned only a single job as its real world counterparts would be. There are only so many times in an operating session that you would want to shuttle hot metal cars from the blast furnace to the open-hearth mixer and back. Tom has solved that problem by assigning 10 different jobs to the

Job title	Union Railroad Clairton works job descriptions
Hot metal transfer	Deliver hot metal cars from blast furnace's hot metal tracks to open-hearth mixer track. Return empty hot metal cars at open hearth to blast furnace. All empty and loaded hot metal cars must be weighed on each run to account for buildup of skull.
Coke-screening station	Take empty hoppers from Ingram Yard to coke-screening station. Pick up loaded coke racks, weigh them, and set them out at Ingram Yard.
Rolling mills	Deliver empty gondolas from Ingram Yard to appropriate track at the rolling mills per waybill. Each track has an identifier that tells the crew where to stop the cars.
Open hearth scrap	Deliver loaded gondolas with scrap from Ingram Yard to open-hearth stockyard.
Coal dump	Deliver loaded hoppers with coal from Ingram Yard to coal dumper at coke works.
Slag run	Swap loaded slag pots at blast furnace and open hearth and replace with empties. Weigh loaded slag pots at scales and then deliver to slag dump at Peters Creek. Return empties to yard.
High line run	Deliver loaded hoppers with limestone and iron ore from Ingram Yard to blast furnace high line. Return empties to Ingram Yard.
Tar loader	Deliver all cars with tar plant waybills to appropriate tracks at the tar plant. Tar, benzene, and creosote all have separate tracks and spots. Return loads to Ingram Yard.
Pig caster run	Pick up loaded hot metal cars at blast furnace and take to pig caster. Return empties to blast furnace after weighing cars.
Ingram Yard job	Pickup and classify all cars from P&WV, P&LE, and PRR interchange tracks. Classify and deliver all outbound cars to the appropriate interchange yards.
Note that Ingram Yard is considered yard limits under control of the yardmaster.	
All mainline trains must stop and get permission to enter Clairton works at the tar plant curve from the Ingram yardmaster.	
Union Railroad mainline job descriptions	
32	Deliver empty coke racks from Duquesne Yard to Clairton works via Ingram Yard.
30	Deliver loaded coke racks from Ingram Yard to Duquesne Yard.
50	Deliver all cars other than coke racks from Duquesne Yard to Ingram Yard.
Ore extra	Deliver loaded ore hoppers from Duquesne Yard to Ingram Yard and return empties.
Mifflin mainline local turn	Starting at Duquesne Yard, switch all industries on Union RR main line in Mifflin and Fisher Auto Body and return to Duquesne Yard.

steel mill operators that they perform more or less sequentially. He usually has two actual crewmen on duty to work the steel mill jobs. One is a yardmaster at Ingram Eastbound Yard, while the other is the switching crew. These two men will work all nine jobs in one operation session (listed in the table on the opposite page), although they rarely have time to finish all the jobs in a typical session.

In addition to the Clairton works-Ingram Yard jobs, the Union Railroad runs five other trains including trains 30 and 32, a coke car transfer run to Duquesne Yard, an ore extra, and a local turn that works industries along the main line.

Tom's lower deck features the P&WV railroad as it traverses the countryside near Pittsburgh, but there is enough operational interest on just this upper deck to make an excellent layout.

5-22

Jeff Bourne's layout features many highly detailed and accurate structure models. *Bob Werre*

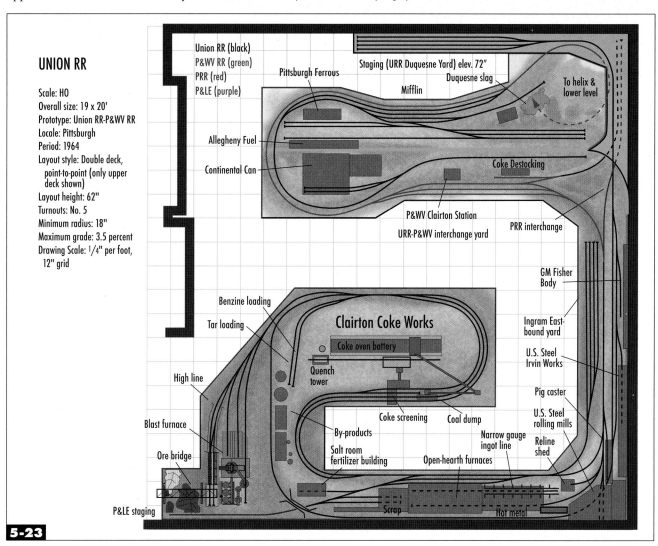

UNION RR

Scale: HO
Overall size: 19 x 20'
Prototype: Union RR-P&WV RR
Locale: Pittsburgh
Period: 1964
Layout style: Double deck, point-to-point (only upper deck shown)
Layout height: 62"
Turnouts: No. 5
Minimum radius: 18"
Maximum grade: 3.5 percent
Drawing Scale: 1/4" per foot, 12" grid

Union RR (black)
P&WV RR (green)
PRR (red)
P&LE (purple)

Pittsburgh Ferrous

Staging (URR Duquesne Yard) elev. 72"
Mifflin
Duquesne slag

To helix & lower level

Allegheny Fuel

Continental Can

Coke Destocking

P&WV Clairton Station
URR-P&WV interchange yard

PRR interchange

GM Fisher Body

Ingram Eastbound yard

U.S. Steel Irvin Works

Benzine loading

Tar loading

Clairton Coke Works

Coke oven battery

Quench tower

Coke screening   Coal dump

High line

By-products

Pig caster

U.S. Steel rolling mills

Blast furnace

Salt room fertilizer building

Narrow gauge ingot line

Reline shed

Ore bridge

Open-hearth furnaces

P&LE staging

Scrap

Hot metal

5-23

Putting it all together

6-1

SIX

Blast furnace L at Sparrows Point mill is the last remaining blast furnace, and it is the focal point of layouts centered around the mill's recent history.

This chapter takes the concepts and ideas presented in the previous five chapters and applies them to designing a steel mill layout based on Bethlehem Steel's Sparrows Point mill, **6-1**. It begins with a detailed look at the history of the mill and then presents three track plans, one N scale and two HO scale.

The sprawling Sparrows Point complex lies about 10 miles outside of Baltimore on the northern tip of Chesapeake Bay, **6-2**. At one time, it was the largest integrated steel mill in the world, and it still sets records for steel production. In 1889, Pennsylvania Steel Company erected the first blast furnaces at Sparrows Point on a low-lying, level piece of ground between Bear Creek and the Patapsco River, a tributary of Chesapeake Bay.

A unique saltwater mill

Sparrows Point has the distinction of being the only deep-water steel mill in the United States. The founders selected this tidewater site to minimize shipping costs on iron ore coming from Cuba and later from Chile. To economically move the ore, the company developed a small fleet of ore ships.

Coal for the furnaces came from West Virginia and Pennsylvania. While some of this coal was conveyed all the way by rail, most of it was carried part of the way by barge and by steamer, as this usually resulted in lower shipping costs. Nearly all the limestone used at Sparrows Point came from the company-owned quarries in Adams County, Pa., about 65 miles away.

The tidewater location caused some problems with water supply. The brackish water of the Chesapeake Bay was unsuitable for the mill's use. Fortunately, the mill was able to tap aquifers deep underground that provided ample freshwater to provide the 500,000 gallons needed per hour.

Along with the mill, the company established a residential community called Sparrows Point, where many workers settled. They enjoyed low rent and free home maintenance, company-subsidized churches and schools, easy access to credit, and a strong sense of community.

At first, the Sparrows Point plant just converted iron ore into pig iron for use in other Pennsylvania Steel plants. In 1891, the company installed Bessemer converters, and Sparrows Point began to produce steel. The mill became fully integrated with coke ovens, a by-product plant, and numerous rolling and blooming mills. Industries developed near the mill to take advantage of the steel production.

Purchased by Bethlehem Steel in 1916, the mill grew in size and capacity, **6-3**. The company expanded capacity seven times between 1916 and 1926. The mill's steel ended up as girders in the Golden Gate Bridge and in cables for the George Washington Bridge.

During World War II, the steel industry underwent a production boom. Bethlehem Steel's mill and the adjacent shipyard, which built cargo and

6-2

Even in the sprawling Sparrows Point complex, corners had to literally be cut to save space.

6-3

As the mill expanded, 12 blast furnaces were built. This is the largest blast furnace to be built at Sparrows Point. All the others have been since torn down. The furnace is largely enclosed, and there is no skip hoist, as the furnace is fed by a conveyor and coal injector.

transport ships, expanded quickly to meet wartime needs.

The postwar years saw continued growth. In 1959, over 35,000 people worked at Sparrows Point, making it the largest employer in Maryland. By this time, facilities for steel production, sheet rolling, pipe fabrication, galvanizing, and shipbuilding and repair, along with ancillary steel-related industries, filled the coastal peninsula, **6-4**.

A surge in steel imports led to massive layoffs among domestic producers, including Bethlehem Steel,

in the 1970s. While the work force declined, through automation and consolidation, steel production continued to grow and reached record levels in 1973.

Modernization continued as a continuous caster went into production in 1974. Later, a massive blast furnace, labeled L, the 12th to be built at the site, replaced several smaller furnaces, **6-5,** while two equally impressive basic oxygen furnaces replaced a large set of open-hearth furnaces, **6-6**. In 1990, the last of the furnaces on blast furnace row

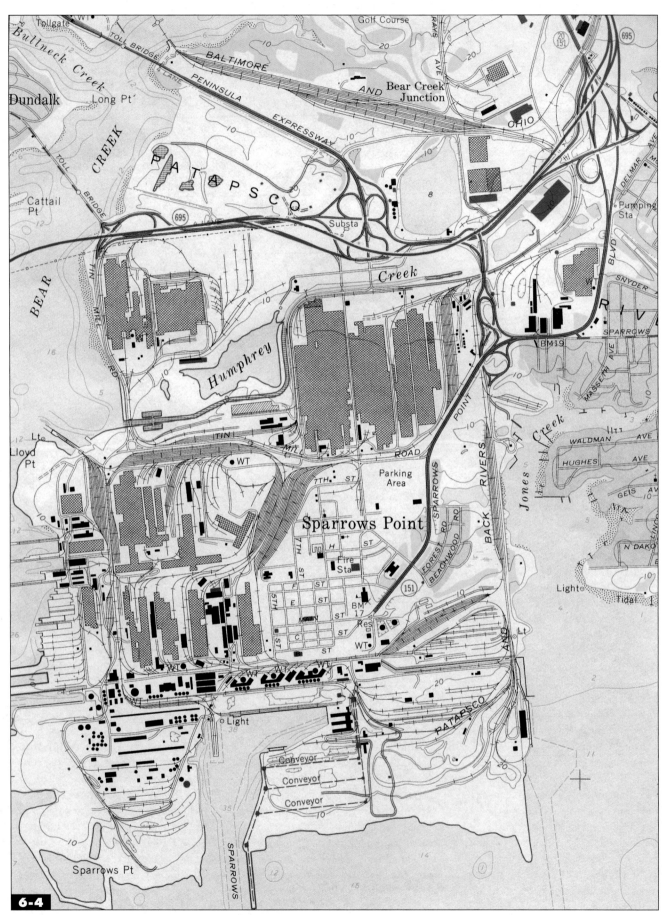

This topographic map of Sparrows Point shows the mill arrangement before blast furnace L was constructed.

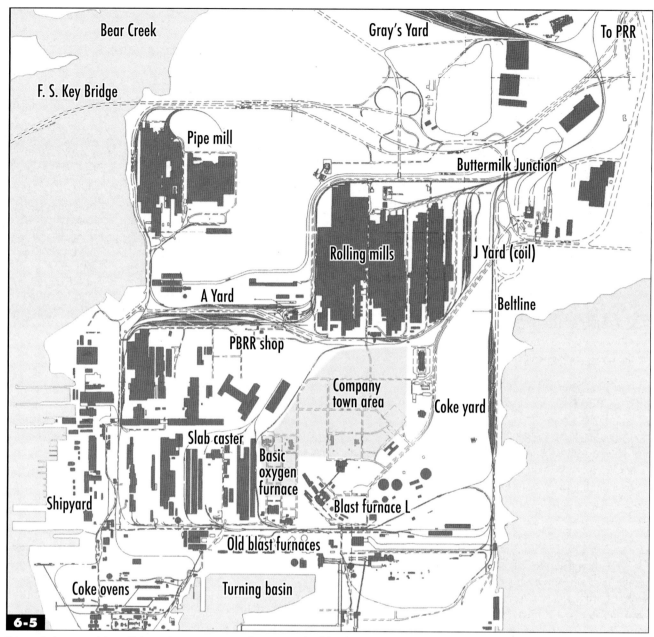

This track diagram of the mill shows the arrangement of structures after blast furnace L was built.

were demolished, leaving only L to make hot metal.

In the 1990s, production slowed. In 1996, the three coke oven batteries were cold idled. Then in 2001, Bethlehem Steel went bankrupt and ownership changed hands several times since then. The mill remains capable of producing 3.9 million tons of steel annually.

Modeling

From a modeling perspective, an appealing aspect of Sparrows Point in the Bethlehem Steel era is that it was served for a long time by four railroads—the Pennsylvania, Baltimore & Ohio, Western Maryland, and Patapsco & Back Rivers. The Western Maryland had no direct connection but relied on barges or trackage rights over the Pennsylvania to deliver limestone from Bittenger, Pa. The Patapsco & Back Rivers Railroad served the mill proper. It was a captive railroad owned by Bethlehem Steel that also handled other customers around the mill. It operated 180 miles of track with 26 locomotives, 9 slugs, and 175 gondolas, as well as a varying number of the 1,700 flatcars in the Bethlehem Steel fleet. The wide variety of motive power and rolling stock adds interest to the

modeling effort, 6-7. Now, Norfolk Southern has replaced the Pennsylvania, and CSX has supplanted the B&O and Western Maryland.

N scale layout design features

A 12 x 12-foot room has adequate space for an N scale layout that uses a hybrid of NTRAK modules and nonmodular sections, 6-8. In this design, the two modular sections (2 x 4 and 3 x 4) are relatively small and easily transportable. They are located in the middle of the room to make removal easier. The modules have no backdrop but instead rely on the large mill structures to

The slab caster (left) and a basic oxygen furnace dominate this view. The basic oxygen furnace replaced open-hearth furnaces. The open end of the slab caster presents interior detail challenges for the modeler. The placards designate various locations for slab storage.

provide a view block. I would also make the rest of the layout in sections to make transportation easier.

The basic plan is essentially an around-the-walls shelf design. However, thanks to the compactness of N scale, there is room for a wye and small helix.

As in the prototype, Gray's Yard is the center of activity. The B&O and WM interchange here with P&BR. The actual Gray's Yard had separate areas for each interchanging railroad. In the prototype, the Pennsylvania Railroad dropped off cars at the Wise Avenue Yard and the P&BR interchanged there. In the layout, there isn't sufficient room for two yards, or even separate areas on the main yard, so all the foreign railroads share arrival/departure tracks and classification tracks. This is a minor concession that should not adversely affect operations.

A double-ended, five-track staging yard resides under Gray's Yard. It can be reached by a one-turn helix on the east end (B&O) and a 4 percent grade on the west end (Pennsylvania Railroad). An optional continuous route for breaking in engines and display purposes could utilize the helix and grade.

The aisles are wide enough to support three or four operators. They also allow access for removing the NTRAK modules.

Operating scheme

Determining an operating scheme first requires selecting an era. The N scale plan models the early 1970s since it was a busy time for the mill. This period also provides a colorful mix of motive power with Chessie and Conrail as the primary connecting railroads and the circus-painted Western Maryland still active. Additional variety in motive power would be available since plenty of Chessie and Conrail predecessor power and cars would still be around as well. The P&BR also painted some of their engines in a colorful bicentennial scheme at this time. More importantly, models of engines from this era are widely available in N scale.

The general operating scheme involves transfer runs from connecting railroads bringing in needed raw materials, supplies, and empties. These trains arrive in Gray's Yard, drop the cars on the arrival/departure tracks, and depart with loads of steel products and empty hoppers.

The P&BR handles all yard switching and classification. Several times daily, the P&BR brings cars from Gray's Yard to switch the various industries on the mill property or nearby locations.

Transfer runs from B&O's Bay View Yard bring coal, alloy materials,

In serving the mill, the P&BR had a large engine house to service and repair its 26 locomotives.

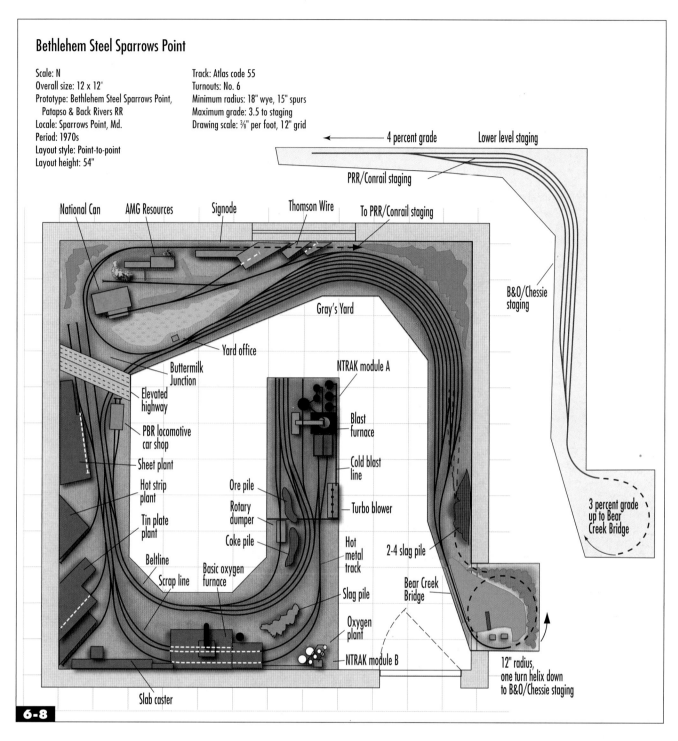

Bethlehem Steel Sparrows Point

Scale: N
Overall size: 12 x 12'
Prototype: Bethlehem Steel Sparrows Point,
    Patapso & Back Rivers RR
Locale: Sparrows Point, Md.
Period: 1970s
Layout style: Point-to-point
Layout height: 54"

Track: Atlas code 55
Turnouts: No. 6
Minimum radius: 18" wye, 15" spurs
Maximum grade: 3.5 to staging
Drawing scale: ⅜" per foot, 12" grid

4 percent grade
Lower level staging
PRR/Conrail staging
To PRR/Conrail staging
B&O/Chessie staging

National Can
AMG Resources
Signode
Thomson Wire

Gray's Yard

Yard office
Buttermilk Junction
Elevated highway
PBR locomotive car shop
Sheet plant
Hot strip plant
Tin plate plant
Beltline
Scrap line
Basic oxygen furnace
Slab caster

NTRAK module A
Blast furnace
Cold blast line
Ore pile
Rotary dumper
Turbo blower
Coke pile
Hot metal track
2-4 slag pile
Slag pile
Bear Creek Bridge
Oxygen plant
NTRAK module B

3 percent grade up to Bear Creek Bridge

12" radius, one turn helix down to B&O/Chessie staging

6-8

supplies, and empties using the Bear Creek Bridge. On the other end, interchange traffic from the PRR's Bay View Yard also continues on to Gray's Yard since the model plan omits the Wise Avenue Yard. The Western Maryland utilizes trackage rights in a similar manner to Conrail although, in this case, the movement is in accordance with prototype operations since Western Maryland's interchange tracks were in Gray's Yard. All these

jobs have short runs from staging to Gray's Yard.

P&BR switchers meet these trains and haul the cars to the classification tracks. In the meantime, the line haulers, after a delay to simulate crew changes, pick up outbound trains and return to staging.

Modeling mill traffic

The blast furnace is a major switching job. Limestone, coke, and ore need to be switched in and empties removed.

Hot metal transfers from the blast furnace to the basic oxygen furnace are a short move and can be omitted or automatically animated. Slag cars get hauled to a slag pit, which I've located behind Gray's Yard.

The basic oxygen furnace also requires a switcher to provide scrap, coke, and small quantities of limestone as well as extracting the empties. With a continuous caster, there are no ingots to move from the basic oxygen furnace

6-9

Various cars wait in the J Yard. Some rolling mill buildings are in the background, and in the foreground, steel slabs on flat cars wait to be moved to the rolling mills.

6-10

A Kress slab carrier rolls through the mill.

6-11

A unit coke train from Bethlehem, Pa., approaches Buttermilk Junction. The Patapsco & Back Rivers Railroad had several slug sets to maximize tractive effort. Note the pile of rusty coils.

to the rolling mills. However, slabs must move from the slab caster to the various rolling mills, 6-9. In modern times, wheeled slab haulers have replaced rail-based flatcars for this task, 6-10.

In the 1970s, coal would move to the coke ovens. Bethlehem Steel cold idled the coke ovens in 1996, so modern modelers should follow Bethlehem Steel's practice of hauling unit trains of coke to Sparrows Point, 6-11. Usually, these arrived every other day for a total of 800 to 1,000 cars per month. Coke moves by conveyor from the coke oven to the blast furnace, so no transfer runs of coke are required, but the empty coal hoppers must be retrieved.

Ore typically arrives by boat at Sparrows Point, but to increase variety, you could add an ore train to the arrivals.

Another job must switch the various rolling mills, 6-12, generally bringing slabs in and taking finished coils out. Some of these coils will move to industries around the mill, but most will leave by way of interchange with a connecting railroad.

For any Western Maryland fan, the operational highlight has to be the daily stone train from Bethlehem Steel's quarry in Bittenger, Pa. This picturesque train usually consisted of gray WM hoppers loaded with crushed limestone, gray covered hoppers with burnt limestone, and empty gondolas and boxcars for finished products. The train would backhaul the empties as well as finished steel products bound for the Western Maryland. In earlier times, this train used a car float from Port Covington, Md., to Sparrows Point but later took an all-land route using trackage rights over the Pennsylvania Railroad. There were infrequent occasions when Bethlehem Steel required great volumes of stone, and the WM ran two stone trains a day. The stone train was very heavy, averaging between 7,000 and 9,000 tons. Usual diesel power consisted of multiple F7s and GP7s and, later, SD35s and SD40s.

During periods of high mill productivity, the WM also hauled out solid slab trains of 100 or more cars. The WM scheduled these trains to avoid the stone train, so only one should operate on the layout at a time.

Local industries

Local industries provide a variety of business for the P&BR. Operators would service these industries with conventional model waybills and car cards.

AMG Resources processes scrap. It receives inbound loads of scrap and an occasional tank car for waste solvents. Outbound gondolas contain processed loads of scrap for the mill. AMG now owns a fleet of high-capacity aluminum gondolas.

Signode Steel Products receives plastic in covered hoppers, chemicals in tank cars, and coils in covered gondolas.

Thomson Wire takes covered gondolas loaded with steel coil and sends out loaded boxcars and scrap.

National Can needs covered gondolas with coil loads, and it ships out boxcars.

This small layout can keep three or four operators busy for several hours. If operations become too familiar, you can spice things up by introducing random events to change the operating conditions. For example, simulating the rebuilding of a facility requires loads of construction material and rerouting of normal traffic. Hot metal loads may be brought in from distant plants while the blast furnace is being relined. These cars receive hotshot priority lest the molten pig iron cools and solidifies, which would ruin the car.

Finally, using a relaxed fast-clock setting like 2:1 or 3:1 lets the crews take time to do the work methodically and in prototypical fashion without rushing. An eight-hour blast cycle could form the basis for an interesting three- to four-hour operating session.

HO layouts

The two HO layouts model an earlier time, before blast furnace L and the basic oxygen furnaces were built and the coke works was still in operation.

One plan utilizes 485 square feet to more accurately model the Sparrows Point operation in the 1950s, in the

6-12

Looking west from the overpass at Buttermilk Junction, the tracks peel off into the rolling mills.

6-13

The open hearth is shown here prior to its demolition.

era before the L blast furnace and the basic oxygen furnace, **6-13**. Thus, the plan includes the impressive row of blast furnaces and the large open hearth, **6-14**. Although the actual mill had four separate open-hearth buildings, the plan shows only one, but it is near scale size. The plan employs some topological liberties to fit even this generous space. For example, the angle of the blast furnace cast houses faces the west instead of the east. This is because the plan omits the coal and coke yard to the east, which would normally provide the tail track to work the blast furnaces. The angled cast houses will require a bit of modification if you start with the Walthers kits. Another distinctive feature is that

most of the Sparrows Point blast furnaces used four stoves. Since the Walthers kit only includes three, some extras will have to be made from tubing or spare kits.

The plan includes three yard areas. The A Yard operators handle the hot end and coke works. The J Yard works the coils and the mill-staging yard. The stockyard's two tracks represent all the other locations in the steel mill and in the shipyard that are not explicitly modeled. Thus, these tracks get finished steel products for the shipyard and slabs for the other rolling mills. In return, this yard would hold empty cars from the shipyard and loads from the rolling mills. So it acts as its own loads in/empties out operation.

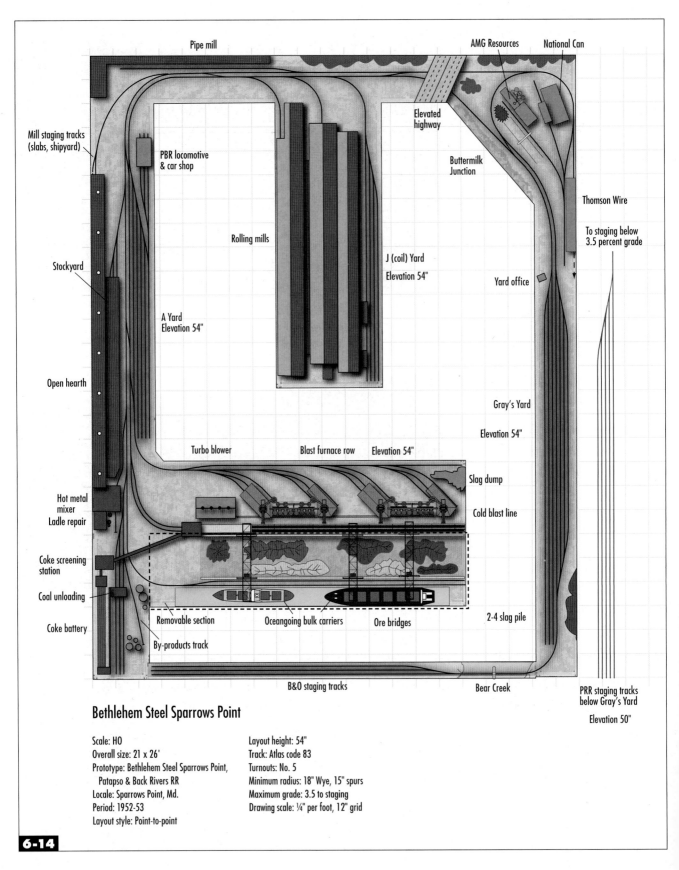

Pipe mill

AMG Resources

National Can

Elevated highway

Mill staging tracks (slabs, shipyard)

PBR locomotive & car shop

Buttermilk Junction

Thomson Wire

Rolling mills

J (coil) Yard
Elevation 54"

Yard office

To staging below
3.5 percent grade

Stockyard

A Yard
Elevation 54"

Open hearth

Gray's Yard

Elevation 54"

Turbo blower

Blast furnace row

Elevation 54"

Slag dump

Hot metal
mixer
Ladle repair

Cold blast line

Coke screening
station

Coal unloading

Coke battery

Removable section

Oceangoing bulk carriers

Ore bridges

2-4 slag pile

By-products track

B&O staging tracks

Bear Creek

PRR staging tracks
below Gray's Yard
Elevation 50"

Bethlehem Steel Sparrows Point

Scale: HO
Overall size: 21 x 26'
Prototype: Bethlehem Steel Sparrows Point,
   Patapso & Back Rivers RR
Locale: Sparrows Point, Md.
Period: 1952-53
Layout style: Point-to-point

Layout height: 54"
Track: Atlas code 83
Turnouts: No. 5
Minimum radius: 18" Wye, 15" spurs
Maximum grade: 3.5 to staging
Drawing scale: ¼" per foot, 12" grid

6-14

The stockyard is hidden under the 16-foot-long open hearth, so this building should be made with removable roof sections to allow access to the tracks, primarily during staging. To avoid opening the roof sections during an operating session, the crew working that yard should just pull or set out long cuts of cars. Once they pull the cars, they take them to the J Yard (or Gray's Yard depending on work load) for switching. There, they would prepare

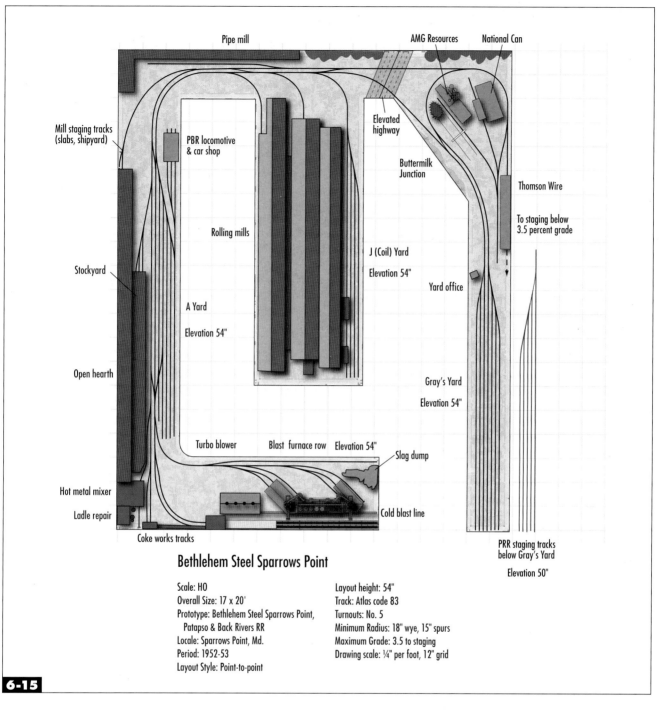

Pipe mill

AMG Resources National Can

Mill staging tracks
(slabs, shipyard)

PBR locomotive
& car shop

Elevated
highway

Buttermilk
Junction

Thomson Wire

Rolling mills

To staging below
3.5 percent grade

Stockyard

J (Coil) Yard
Elevation 54"

Yard office

A Yard

Elevation 54"

Open hearth

Gray's Yard

Elevation 54"

Turbo blower   Blast furnace row   Elevation 54"

Slag dump

Hot metal mixer

Cold blast line

Ladle repair

Coke works tracks

PRR staging tracks
below Gray's Yard

Elevation 50"

Bethlehem Steel Sparrows Point

Scale: HO
Overall Size: 17 x 20'
Prototype: Bethlehem Steel Sparrows Point,
    Patapso & Back Rivers RR
Locale: Sparrows Point, Md.
Period: 1952-53
Layout Style: Point-to-point

Layout height: 54"
Track: Atlas code 83
Turnouts: No. 5
Minimum Radius: 18" wye, 15" spurs
Maximum Grade: 3.5 to staging
Drawing scale: ¼" per foot, 12" grid

6-15

the set-outs for the return run, classified by station (switching order) to make the job more interesting.

As in the N scale plan, the Gray's Yard switcher services some of the industries past Buttermilk Junction. The B&O accesses Gray's Yard from its own three-track staging yard, while the PRR staging yard is below Gray's Yard and is reached by a inclined ramp.

Like the Rouge Steel plan (page 67), this plan includes a large area devoted to the ore yard and waterfront. Since

this is a tidewater steel mill, and not on the Great Lakes, any ship docked here will be oceangoing. Because there is only a single track along the waterfront pier, it would not be difficult to make this section of the layout removable for maintenance or access. The dotted lines in the track plan show a suggested joint location for making the removable section. It could be mounted on casters or skids to allow easy access.

If you are not as dedicated a ship modeler as a steel mill modeler, the

plan shown in figure **6-15** omits that interesting section of the layout. It also reduces blast furnace row by half, which results in a smaller layout (340 square feet) that should easily fit in a two-car garage. The plan retains much of the operational potential of the larger plan except in the coke works, where only two stub tracks represent that facility. The B&O and PRR share the staging tracks under Gray's Yard with a corresponding reduction in capacity.

Modeling techniques

7-1

SEVEN

This overall view of the completed blast furnace shows the skip hoist side with a train pulling a cut of cars on the high line.

Now that we have looked at lots of theory and design concepts, it's time to put them into practice. This chapter discusses some techniques that you can use in building structures and railcars for your steel mill. First, I'll describe some of the construction techniques that I used to modify the HO Walthers kits for use on my N scale Alkem Steel NTRAK module. I will not give a detailed step-by-step description since I suspect that few of you will copy these structures exactly. Instead, I'll cover the main points and describe the thoughts behind the modifications. I used similar construction techniques for the rolling mill and the open-hearth structures. Most of these techniques apply in any scale.

This close-up shows the open hearth on the left and the rolling mill on the right with its roof made from Evergreen corrugated siding. Note the cooling fan detail (center) added to help provide scale reference to the structure.

Walthers now offers its rolling mill kits in N scale. If you use those kits, you can skip some of the steps I have included. Even though the N scale kits are available, the HO kit, when used in an N scale application, makes a very impressive and close to prototype-sized structure.

Then, I'll go over how to detail the Walthers blast furnace kit, **7-1**, and finish with some painting tips for weathering steel mill slag cars and hot metal cars.

Rolling mill building

I used three of the Walthers HO rolling mill kits for this structure, which is 42" long, about 8" tall, and 6" deep. Before building, I mocked up the structure. It's easy to do by temporarily assembling the wall sections using masking tape. I tried various configurations and made several perspective drawings to determine the final shape.

Before assembling the kits, I reduced the height of the steel siding panels in the kits to a more appropriate N scale size. I scribed lines halfway between

each simulated steel panel. While this is tedious, it goes quickly if you use a spacing jig. Make sure you keep the scribed lines parallel to the existing seam lines. It goes much easier by applying very light pressure using the back of a hobby-knife blade. Too much scribing pressure tends to make the knife point wander. You can skip this step if you are using the kits on their respective scale layouts.

I glued the wall sections together using several pieces of spare plastic to reinforce each joint and to brace the corners to keep them square. I did not use the internal kit trusses since they would not be visible in the enclosed structure.

I built the roof with Evergreen corrugated siding and added a back wall to provide strength, **7-2**. I lowered the walls of the main part of the structure about an inch. I used the leftover piece from this cut to construct the bump-out for the craneway. The cross gable on the right-hand side came from a leftover end wall. To maximize

the length of the structure, I notched the right-hand side to allow room for the return loop track. A steel I-beam and a column help support the cantilevered corner of the structure. I copied this feature from a prototype structure at Sparrows Point (see photo 6-2).

The Walthers kits come with two types of ventilators. For this structure, I used the cylindrical roof ventilators, **7-3**. The craneway and cross gable helped break up the structure's mass, but more detail was needed to scale down the structure. I added several small N scale structures along the front of the building to provide visual N scale references. I scratchbuilt an air-cooling system, complete with fan blades and Micromesh screens to match a prototype I saw at Sparrows Point, **7-4**. I built a one-story loading dock and office annex by using DPM components, **7-5**. Reference photos showed numerous pipes running along the outside of these structures, so I added Plastruct and Evergreen tubing to simulate stacks and piping.

7-3

I used cylindrical roof ventilators for this structure, and the letters for the sign came from an office supply store. The slab crane is a modified Kibri container crane.

7-4

The scratchbuilt fans, varied roof lines, cross gables, industrial clutter, and heavy weathering add interest to this view of the rolling mill.

7-5

I built the loading dock and office annex from DPM components and added tubing to simulate piping.

An open shed covers the stockyard tracks by the open hearth. I made the shed of leftover truss pieces from the rolling mills and a sheet-siding roof.

This detail shot is of one of the blast furnaces at Ford's Rouge Steel mill. I copied the truss arrangement on my furnace.

The craneway has a platform on the right-hand side with some N scale handrails and ladders. I made the sign on the roof using letters from an office supply store, a Plastruct truss, and leftover pieces from the kits' trusses.

Open-hearth furnace

The open hearth provided its own set of challenges. First off, prototype open hearths are very large structures with many support tracks. You could nearly make a layout just by modeling the trackwork associated with an open hearth. Massive selective compression would be required to fit the structure into the 32 inches I had available.

Secondly, in my plan, the open hearth straddled the module joint. To simplify module teardown and assembly at shows, I decided to build a base for the structure that included the tracks. In effect, the open hearth itself is a mini-module. Three screws secure the structure to the module, and a wiring harness with Cinch-Jones plugs electrically connects the tracks.

I cut ¼" foam core panels to the appropriate shape and built a solid-walled inner structure. Then, using a hot glue gun, I sided the inner structure with panels from the kits. I braced the interior of the structure in several places, most importantly along the roof apex and wall corners. This construction technique produced a strong building that could withstand the rigors of traveling to shows. As a bonus, it freed up all the trusses and columns that came with the kits. I later assembled these trusses and roofed them with Evergreen corrugated siding to create open shed structures, which I placed around the open hearth. The multiple roof lines helped add depth to the scene.

A row of tall chimneys, one associated with each furnace, characterizes an open-hearth structure. To accurately follow a typical prototype in my 32-inch space, I should have had three of these stacks. However, I took some artistic license and doubled this number to six. The stacks connect to a shed-like addition across the front of the main structure.

Two HO scale Walthers rolling mill kits built to their full size make up the main structure. The gabled sides have openings to allow the three staging tracks to pass through. On the rooftop, I used monitor vents (the other venting option in the kit). I added a shed to the left front to house the mixer building. Here, the molten pig iron pours into a mixer that charges the open hearths. To simulate the fireworks that occur in this shed when iron is poured, I added a set of blinking lights from a Model Power kit originally designed to simulate a burning building.

An open shed in the front of the open hearth covers the stockyard tracks, **7-6**. The stockyard stores scrap loaded in gondolas for processing. As mentioned, the trusses for this shed are from the kits. The elevated line is simply a 1 x 2 piece of wood with a section of flextrack glued to the top and strip styrene glued to the sides to simulate concrete beams. In an actual stockyard, the elevated rail line would lead into the structure. I omitted this track in my plan. I modified a Walthers HO traveling crane to fit on the crane tracks inside the shed.

7-8

Alkem Steel engine no. 2 pulls mill gondolas past the blast furnace, with details such as the gas washer and extra piping added.

Detailing the Walthers blast furnace

The blast furnace is the signature structure of any steel mill, **7-7**. Prior to 1996, modelers that wanted a blast furnace had to scratchbuild one. It is a complex structure with several parts that are hard to scratchbuild, especially the furnace shaft. In spite of this, several talented modelers such as Dean Freytag, Jeff Bourne, Ken McCorry, and Logan Holtgrewe have built notable

examples. When Walthers released its blast furnace model, building a blast furnace became much easier.

As good as the Walthers kit is, it can benefit from extra detailing, and I will describe how I detailed an N scale kit, **7-8**. Walthers introduced an improved version of the HO kit in 2009, and it includes some of the details (notably stairs) that I had to add to my N scale model. Many of the details that I added to the N scale model would also apply

to the HO model, and I will try to point out differences where they exist. For more comprehensive step-by-step guidance on detailing an HO blast furnace, you can follow Jeff Bourne's videos (see page 6).

When Walthers released the blast furnace kit, the design was selectively compressed to allow the blast furnace to fit in a reasonable space on a layout. So how much was it compressed? It depends!

The height of a blast furnace is limited by the strength of the coke used in it. Taller furnaces with taller columns of material inside put more weight on the coke at the bottom. If the weight is too great, the coke will crush, which prevents the blast air from passing through the furnace and stops the ore reduction. As researchers came up with stronger forms of coke, steel mill designers were able to make taller furnaces. In fact, all the dimensions of a blast furnace tend to be tailored for the type and form of ore and coke used. For example, a furnace that uses pelletized ore has a different profile than one that uses straight ore. Furnace profiles were frequently rebuilt to accommodate changes in raw materials. This inflexibility is one of the great disadvantages of a blast furnace.

Once steel-shaft furnaces came into service in the late 19th century, blast furnaces rapidly grew in size. By 1910, most furnaces were at least 80 feet tall from iron notch to the top of the shaft. Figure **7-9** shows the progression in blast-furnace shaft dimensions from 1911 through 1978. The Walthers HO and N scale furnaces are included for comparison. Furnace sizes did not grow much taller once they reached the 120-foot mark in 1929 because of the coke-crushing issue. Modern furnaces increase production by having a wider hearth, multiple tapholes, and higher blast velocities. The figure shows that the Walthers N scale furnace is right on the money for a 1940s design. At 77 scale feet tall, the HO kit is too small. By how much depends on the era. Around 1910, it is only about 25 percent too small, but it is nearly 35 percent too small in representing a furnace from the 1940s onward.

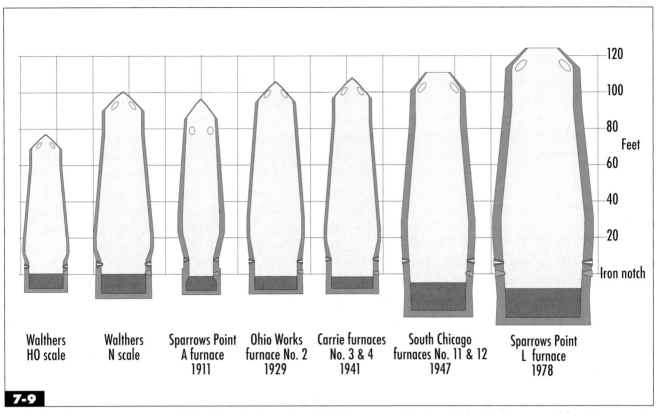

| 120 |
| 100 |
| 80 Feet |
| 60 |
| 40 |
| 20 |
| Iron notch |

Walthers HO scale · Walthers N scale · Sparrows Point A furnace 1911 · Ohio Works furnace No. 2 1929 · Carrie furnaces No. 3 & 4 1941 · South Chicago furnaces No. 11 & 12 1947 · Sparrows Point L furnace 1978

7-9

The scale height of Walthers HO and N blast furnace kits are compared here to prototype furnaces. The heights are measured from the iron notch.

Another factor to consider when detailing a blast furnace is that the top-works evolved over time. A common early design featured each uptake with its own stack (figure 2-11). Later furnaces exhibit top-works that extend vertically. The top-works of the Walthers kit has a later design. They also tend to have double-wishbone style uptakes with a single downcomer as in the Walthers kit. Blast furnace L at Sparrows Point has a huge set of offtakes that tower to 285 feet above the dual tapholes. The Sloss-Sheffield furnaces (see photo 5-2) stand about 84 feet tall and are about 10 percent larger in scale than the Walthers kit. But the Sloss-Sheffield furnaces had very simplified top-works compared to later furnaces. To make a convincing model of the Sloss-Sheffield furnaces, you could use the Walthers shaft and scratchbuild the top-works, a task made easier by the simplified design.

Several modelers, including Chuck Pravlik, have backdated the Walthers HO furnace by building the offtakes to an earlier design, **7-10**. Others combine Walthers kit parts with a larger scratchbuilt furnace shaft and

downcomer. The N scale kit can be built without any concern about furnace size.

Building tips

The blast furnace is a big, complex kit. It will take you some time to get used to the parts and locate them on the sprues. To simplify the parts hunt, I found it useful to discard a sprue once all the parts were off.

The kit generally uses a split-pipe design for most cylindrical parts such as piping, furnace shafts, stoves, and other items. You could use plastic tubing or wooden dowels to avoid the need to build up and fill the seams on all these parts. But not all the kit parts have exact matches for available tubing, so you need to plan ahead if you decide to replace the split pipes. For this build, I used kit parts for some and plastic tubing in others, depending on the particular application.

Large-diameter pipes typically found in a steel mill present a dilemma for steel mill constructors. In the prototype, it is very difficult and expensive to cast or form large-diameter elbows or curved pipes. Instead, mitered straight seg-

ments are welded together. This process creates a distinctive look to the pipe curves. To replicate this, I used my 12" chop saw to carefully cut precise 10- and 15-degree segments to build up my mitered elbows, **7-11**. A smaller miter saw would work for these tiny parts, but the chop saw is what I had available. Be careful when using such a saw to cut small parts. Keep your fingers away from the blade by using clamps and push sticks.

Even straight lengths of pipe were made with individual segments. To simulate this with plastic tubing, I used various methods to scribe simulated weld lines on my pipes. These techniques included using a hose clamp to guide the back of a hobby knife blade for larger-diameter pipes, **7-12**, and using a K&S mini pipe cutter to scribe the lines for smaller pipes, **7-13**.

I had a little difficulty in aligning the walls of the furnace cast house. This happened because I built the frame first and months later tried to glue on the walls. It would have been easier to build the cast house as a single assembly and square it up while the glue and joints were still flexible.

7-10

Chuck Pravlik backdated a Walthers blast furnace with new uptakes and a variety of other piping. *Chuck Pravlik*

The Walthers kit does a good job of providing the primary piping. An actual blast furnace has many more secondary pipes for regulating flows and then another layer of smaller-diameter pipes used for cooling water and electrical conduits. Modern furnaces also have sensors on nearly every valve and pipe section with wires running to them. Trying to capture all of these parts and wires is a modeling challenge on the same magnitude as rigging a clipper ship, except no real documentation is available. You have to rely on prototype photos and some engineering judgment of what is feasible.

I detailed the furnace shaft but was restrained from going all out as this part is very difficult to see once the kit is assembled, **7-14**. I added two walkways and a hint of cooling pipes to the tuyeres. I painted the furnace shaft a dark, rusty color, but once it was installed in the model, I went back and drybrushed it heavily with lighter colors, so some of the details can be seen in the dim light.

For this detailing project, I made some of the parts in clear acrylic and cut them with a laser cutter. This saves time in making multiple cuts, but you can achieve the same results with hand-cut styrene.

The top-works is a highly visible part of the model, so I spent a lot of time detailing it, **7-15**. I used prototype photos, such as 7-7, as inspiration. I

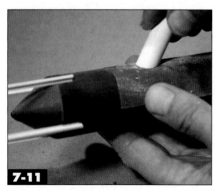

7-11

To make a coped joint when adding pipes, wrap one tube with sandpaper and rub it against another until you have the desired curve.

7-12

To scribe weld lines on the stack, I used an adjustable hose clamp as a guide when scribing with the back of a hobby-knife blade.

7-13

On the smaller gas mains, I scribed weld lines with a K&S pipe cutter. Be careful not to cut the pipe in half.

7-14

Detailing the furnace shaft is an exercise in hidden work as this part is hard to see when installed in the kit.

7-15

The highly visible top-works received a lot of detailing attention, such as adding stairways, which are a painstaking but vital detail.

7-16

The completed top-works includes detailing that simulates double bell controls, such as telescoping tubes.

added stairs and telescoping tubes for the double bells, **7-16** (also figure 2-16). The trolley crane came from bits of scrap parts and a small hook made from a piece of wire, **7-17**. In retrospect, I would have built a single-work platform instead of the multiple platforms that I added because it was harder to do and there was little noticeable difference.

I followed information in Jeff Bourne's videos to modify and detail the dust catcher and gas washers, **7-18**. I rerouted some of the kit piping, but this is not necessary as I found prototype photos showing the stock kit arrangement too.

Goggle valves are very prominent in this part of the blast furnace. I used Alkem Scale Models goggle valves to speed construction of these time-consuming detail parts, **7-19**. I also used Alkem Scale Models gate valves on the stoves and burners.

The kit's high line is quite simple and benefits from extra work, **7-20**. I made

sloped hopper bins from sheet styrene, **7-21**. I also added corrugated walls to the fronts that I cut to match the slots inside the vertical H-beams. For the high line, I built appropriately sized boxes from sheet styrene and painted them a concrete color. Once I had these assembled, I added flextrack to them, but when the model is installed, I plan to replace it with track laid directly on the concrete. I used Alkem Scale Models handrails to detail the high line and numerous other locations on the model, **7-22**.

The cast house floor is the business end of the blast furnace, and I added

7-17

I scratchbuilt a small trolley crane for the top-works from pieces of scrap material and a hook fashioned of wire.

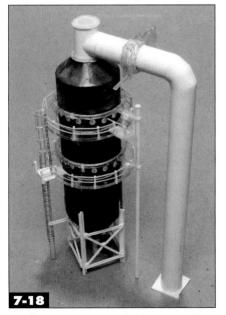

7-18

I made some new piping for the gas washer following Jeff Bourne's videos. Using Walthers piping is also an option.

7-19

This is an unpainted Alkem Scale Models goggle valve designed for use with the Walthers HO blast furnace kit.

7-20

The kit's high line is simplified. I embellished the center steel sections with sets of sloped hoppers, a scratchbuilt hoist house, and high-line extensions made with sheet styrene to simulate concrete.

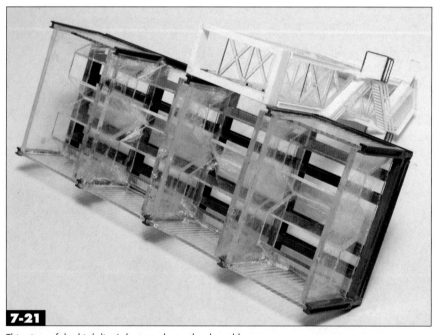

7-21

This view of the high line's bottom shows the sloped hoppers.

7-22

I added a set of etched ladders with safety cages (Gold Medal Models) to the stack. I replaced all the kit handrails with laser-cut handrails (Alkem Scale Models).

some details to make it more accurate. These details included a mud gun and tap drill made from scrap pieces, **7-23** and **7-24**. I laser-cut the gates, skimmers, runner plates, and overhead crane, **7-25** and **7-26**. I sprinkled some cinders on the cast house floor and drybrushed them when dry to simulate the sand and dirt that accumulates. Photo 2-8 provides additional detailing ideas.

The completed model makes an impressive structure, **7-27**. There is still much more you could to do to detail it, such as adding lights, more rigging, and pipes—lots of pipes, **7-28**. Use prototype photos for ideas and have at it.

Painting

I tried to paint the parts as I built them. This resulted in the subassemblies having slightly different shades and hues since I used different color mixes each time. When the model was mostly assembled, I went back with my airbrush and paintbrushes to repaint and weather the parts, so they blended together.

7-23

7-24

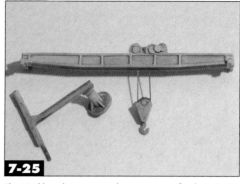
7-25

The mud gun is an important detail in the cast house. I scratchbuilt mine from plastic and acrylic scrap pieces.

The tap drill was a simple scratchbuilt item. I painted the tap drill and trolley crane yellow to make them more visible (photo 7-25).

The Walthers kit comes with a craneway for the cast house but no crane. A Walthers N scale trolley crane is too big for this application, so I made one from scratch.

7-26

I made one of the cast house roof panels removable to afford a better view of the cast house interior. The steel plates partially covering the runners are based on the ones seen in photo 2-8. Note the gates and skimmers, which are other important details.

Speaking of painting, I tend to use a base color of flat black and red oxide primer, sprayed on top of each other in quick successive coats when they are still wet. Then I lightly spray on Rust-Oleum Earth Brown Camouflage, dusting the parts from the top. Later, I use my airbrush to apply more blending colors. I like to use Vallejo Model Air Black,

Dark Earth, Camouflage Light Brown, and Mahagony (Vallejo's spelling) in a Badger 360 airbrush with a small paint cup. This airbrush is easy to clean and allows rapid changes of color, which is perfect for weathering and detail painting. I also used Polly Scale Grimy Black, Roof Brown, and Mineral Red diluted about 50-50 with acrylic thinner.

For dry brushing, I use Ceramcoat craft acrylics: Red Oxide, Black, Pumpkin Orange, Spice Brown (a great color available in larger sizes as I use a lot of it), Clay Bisque (a good color for concrete), Burnt Umber, and Burnt Sienna. I can't describe any particular formula. I tend to mix and add colors as

(continued on page 92)

7-27

The overall view of the completed blast furnace offers an impressive sight.

7-28

I added a long extension to the cold blast line and a goggle valve to control it. Eventually I plan to add a second blast furnace, and this pipe will connect to it and the turbo blower building.

7-29

Walthers offers preassembled and painted hot metal cars and slag cars. You just have to add wire grabs. I added a base coat of red oxide and black primer, but it doesn't completely cover the green base.

7-30

This smoking hot metal car is the prototype example I used when weathering my car, including the numbers and lettering.

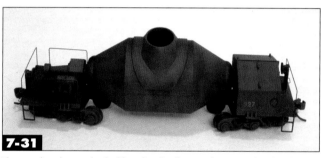

7-31

This is what the car looks like after the first application of airbrushed weathering. I used darker colors to bring out the shadows.

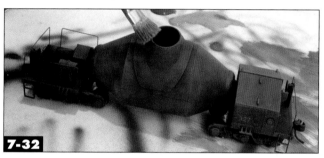

7-32

Drybrushing brings out some of the highlights and details.

7-33

Next, to capture the look of the prototype car, I dappled the car with rust, spice brown, and orange using an old paintbrush.

7-34

To simulate skull, I used thick cyanoacrylate adhesive covered with black N scale cinder ballast. Then I painted the skull flat black and drybrushed it with light gray.

7-35

As a finishing touch to this car, I applied graffiti lettering that I copied from the prototype.

7-36

I weathered a slag car in a similar manner but brushed on white acrylic paint to simulate lime.

7-37

I also weathered some Magarac N scale hot metal cars (top) and Overland brass slag cars.

7-38

This side-by-side view of the weathered HO and N scale hot metal cars shows similar results.

(continued from page 89)

I see fit, but I rarely use any color straight. I think this comes from years of experience painting many materials in many scales.

Weathering hot metal cars and slag cars

I have always enjoyed weathering my models. It's a great way to hide mistakes made during construction, and it allows you to add play value to a model. Even assembled and painted kits can—and should be—weathered, **7-29**, which is what I did with factory assembled and painted Walthers slag cars and hot metal cars and several N scale car kits.

I photographed a hot metal car working at Ford's Rouge Steel mill in 2003, **7-30**. The smoking car really caught my attention. I used this car to guide the weathering process even

though it is not an exact match for my model car.

The first step was spraying a light base coat of red oxide and black primer on the model, trying to let some of the base color show. Since this is a heavily weathered car, I covered most of the green factory color. I didn't bother to remove the wheelsets. I later cleaned the wheel tread with a wire brush in my motor tool. Once the primer dried, I airbrushed various browns and reds and black to simulate rust and streaking, **7-31**. Then I drybrushed the raised model edges with a mixture of orange and spice brown to bring out details, **7-32**. The final step was dappling (or stippling) various shades of orange and brown to simulate rust colors, **7-33**. I applied the paint in light layers and let it dry before applying more layers. By building up a few layers like this, the effect is more realistic.

To simulate the skull around the pouring spout, I applied thick cyanoacrylate adhesive (CA) using a toothpick, a trick I learned from Jim Hediger. Gravity caused the glue to run slightly as I sprinkled black N scale cinders on it. Once it had the shape I wanted, I hit it with CA accelerator. Then, using the same process, I added one or two more applications to simulate multiple splashes. I touched up the skull with black paint and then drybrushed the top with light gray to bring out the individual grains, **7-34**. Finally, I hand-painted the lettering, trying to match the letters of the original, **7-35**.

The HO slag car received a similar treatment, except that instead of adding skull, I drybrushed white paint to simulate lime, **7-36**.

The same techniques worked for the N scale cars as well. The cinder pots are Overland Brass models while the hot metal cars are resin kits from Magarac Models, **7-37**. I added Z scale couplers to the cinder pots because N scale couplers wouldn't fit. Even with Z scale couplers, I had to grind away the brass coupler boxes. I drilled holes through the frames and used small screws to hold the couplers in place. I added metal wheelsets to the hot metal cars. Once the cars were weathered, they compared favorably to their HO cousins, **7-38**.

Glossary

Bag house: A facility used for industrial dust collection and pollution control.

Basic oxygen furnace: A steel refiner in which molten pig iron and steel scrap convert to steel from the oxidizing action of oxygen blown into the melt under a basic (nonacidic) slag.

Bessemer process: A method for making steel by blasting compressed air through molten iron to burn out excess carbon and impurities. Named after its developer Henry Bessemer.

Billet: A section of steel used for rolling into bars, rods, and sections produced directly by continuous casting or by casting ingots.

Blast furnace: A furnace in which coke and iron ore react together under a hot airflow to form liquid hot metal or pig iron.

Bloom: A large square section of steel, intermediate in the rolling process between an ingot and a billet. Blooms are produced by continuous casting, which eliminates the necessity of first producing an ingot.

Blower: An air compressor or pump.

Bottle car: A cylindrical car specially designed to haul molten iron or steel. The cylinder rotates to empty the contents. Also called a submarine or torpedo car.

Bulk carrier: A ship designed to carry loose, granular cargo such as coal, grain, or ore.

By-product plant: Area of a coke manufacturing plant that recovers useful products from the exhaust gas of the coke-making process.

Cast house: The part of the blast furnace where molten iron is either cast into pig iron or routed to bottle cars.

Cinder notch: A taphole in a blast furnace for molten slag.

Cinder pot: A specialized car that carries molten slag.

Coke: The mostly carbon solid residue obtained from coal and other carbonaceous materials after removal of volatile material by destructive distillation. It is used as a fuel and in making steel.

Coke battery: The arrangement of ovens used to make coke.

Carbon electrode: A nonmetal electric conductor consisting of carbon or a graphite rod used in an electric arc furnace.

Continuous casting: A process in which molten steel is poured into a mold where it takes on a solid form and flows to a cutter in a single strand. The slab is cut to a required length and processed further.

Craneway: A portion of a structure where an overhead crane can travel.

Degass: A process to remove gas from molten iron or steel.

Dust catcher: A device that collects dust from a furnace or exhaust gas.

Electric arc furnace: A furnace in which an electric current provides the source of heat for making steel.

Finishing mill: A rolling mill in which sheet, plate, and other mill products undergo final rolling.

Flux: A substance added to metals while they are in a furnace to remove impurities.

Goggle valve: A valve used to shut off the flow of gas in a gas main or in a duct. The valve plate has two equal circular areas that resemble a giant pair of eye goggles.

High line: An elevated rail line that serves the skip hoist of a blast furnace.

Home scrap: Scrap steel or iron generated at the steel mill.

Hot-metal ladle: A large bucket-shaped container for transferring molten metal.

Hulett unloader: A power device that employs an articulated arm and traversing bed to remove bulk materials from a ship's cargo hold.

Ingot casting: The process of pouring molten metal into separate molds until the metal solidifies into ingots.

Glossary (continued)

Integrated steel mill: A iron-working facility that takes raw materials in the form of ore, coal, and scrap and produces finished steel products.

Iron ore: Rocks or minerals containing compounds from which iron can be refined.

Lance: A water-cooled probe that injects oxygen into a furnace or hot-metal car.

Larry car: A specialized railcar that loads coal into a coke oven.

Mini-mill: A steelmaking facility where an electric arc furnace is the primary steel refiner and uses mostly scrap instead of pig iron.

Mixer: A refractory-lined tilting drum that stores and combines batches of hot metal to even out irregularities in their composition.

Open-hearth furnace: A steelmaking furnace in which the steel is placed on a shallow hearth and flames of burning gas and hot air pass over it.

Ore bridge: A large traveling crane mounted on fixed rails and built using a steel truss.

Ore transfer car: A specialized railcar that loads raw materials into a skip-hoist hopper.

Pig iron: The product of a blast furnace. The term was derived from the method of casting pig-iron bars in depressions or molds formed in the sand floor adjacent to the furnace. When filled with metal, the connecting runner (known as a sow) and numerous smaller molds resembled a litter of suckling pigs.

Post-consumer scrap: Scrap steel from recycled commercial products.

Prompt scrap: Scrap metal generated by metal-working and fabrication industries that includes turnings, cutting, punchings, and borings.

Quench car: A specialized railcar that takes hot coke from the coke oven to the quenching tower.

Refractory brick: A ceramic material used in lining furnaces, kilns, fireboxes, and fireplaces that has a melting point well above the operating temperatures of the process.

Runner: A channel through which molten metal is poured into a mold.

Sinter: Forms a bonded mass by heating metal powders without melting.

Skull: The cooled residue of spilled hot metal or slag that builds up on objects.

Slab: A semi-finished steel product that is converted into sheet and strip products at the rolling mill.

Slag: A by-product from the manufacture of steel using pig iron.

Slag ladle: A large bucket-shaped container for transferring molten slag.

Soaking pit: A high-temperature, gas-fired, tightly covered, refractory-lined hole or pit into which a hot metal ingot is held at a fixed temperature until it is needed for rolling into sheet or other forms.

Steel: An iron alloy containing small amounts of carbon.

Stove: A facility having refractory bricks arranged in a checkered pattern that burns gas and stores heat.

Strip: Removing a mold from an ingot.

Tap a blast furnace: Opening a hole in the side of a blast furnace to allow molten iron or slag to pour out.

Teem: Pouring liquid steel from a ladle to fill a mold with molten metal.

Tundish: A receptacle used in metal foundries to hold molten metal, usually in the continuous casting process.

Tuyere: A tube, nozzle, or pipe through which air is blown into a furnace or hearth.

Wrought iron: An iron alloy having a very low carbon content when compared to steel. Widely used in the past, it was supplanted by steel for structural purposes, and its use has become principally decorative.

About the author

Bernard Kempinski is a freelance writer who has written more than 40 magazine articles on model railroading, many of them on layout planning, and one book on realistic, midsize track plans. He is an active model railroader and has built many models on commission, including a 1950s steel mill and a paper mill featured in recent Walthers catalogs. A former U.S. Army captain, Bernard works as a defense analyst in Washington, D.C.

Dedication

My wife, Alicia, is due special recognition for her unfailing support, encouragement, and understanding during the preparation of this project.

Acknowledgements

I would like to thank the following individuals for their help in preparing this book:

First, Mark Thompson at Kalmbach for his confidence and patience, Jeff Wilson for locating photos in Kalmbach's David P. Morgan Memorial Library, and Randy Rehberg for editing the book.

Mac Beard of the C&O Historical Society, Eric Craig, Paul Dolkos, Roger Durfree, Stephen Faust, Gary Gealy, Tom Habak, Jim Hediger, Mark Hemphill, Joel Hinkhouse, Ron Lane, J. Alex Lang, Ken Larsen, Mike Mautner, Chuck Pravlik, Chris Schmuck, Ted Schnef, Siemens AG, Bill Stephens, and Bob Werre for providing photos.

Darius Chagnon, Eric Craig, Jim Hediger, Ken McCorry, Mike Pennie, Monroe Stewart, and Tom Wilson for use of their track plans.

Kara Benson and Bob Gallegos of Walthers for their support and the excellent model kits that make steel mill modeling so much easier.

Professor Steve Semken of Arizona State University for assisting with information on the origin of iron ore.

Mark Andersen, John Drye, and Len White for their last-minute help.

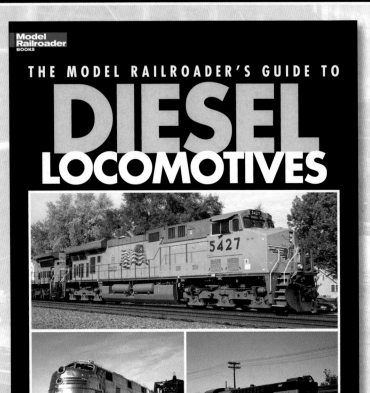

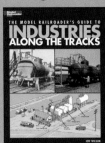

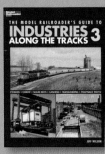